P9-DHP-253

To

From

Date

Scriptures and Meditations *for* Your *Best Life* Now

JOEL OSTEEN

NEW YORK · BOSTON · NASHVILLE

Literary development and design: Koechel Peterson & Associates, Inc., Minneapolis, Minnesota.

Portions of this book have been adapted from *Your Best Life Now*, copyright © 2004 and *Daily Readings from Your Best Life Now*, copyright © 2005 by Joel Osteen. Published by Warner Faith.

FaithWords
Hachette Book Group USA
1271 Avenue of the Americas, New York, NY 10020
Visit our Web site at www.faithwords.com.

The FaithWords name and logo are trademarks of Hachette Book Group, USA.

Printed in the United States of America.
First Printing: October 2006
10 9 8 7 6 5 4 3 2 1
ISBN-10: 0-446-58065-6-1
ISBN-13: 978-0-446-57827-1
Library of Congress Control Number: 2006930301

Table of Contents

Introduction

Since the publication of *Your Best Life Now*, millions of people have been discovering what it means to live happy, successful, fulfilled lives. The answer lies in a simple yet profound process to change the way you think about your life and help you accomplish what's truly important. It starts with the understanding that the future begins with what happens in your life today. As we make the most of the present moment, we build our future one day at a time.

If you're like me, you don't want to live your life with a "barely-get-by" mentality. You want to crack the ordinary mold and become the best you can be. You want to break the power of the past and the chains of limitations and feelings of inadequacy. You want to learn how to live your best life now and discover the joy, peace, and enthusiasm that God has for you.

In this book, you will discover just how to do that! Allow the Scriptures to speak to you. Be still and listen to what God is saying through His words. Explore what it means to enlarge your vision. Learn what God has to say about you and allow Him to rebuild your self-image. Understand the power of your thoughts and words, and begin to let go of the past. Renew your strength despite whatever adversity you face. Learn to live as a person who gives generously without reservations, and choose to be happy.

If you take these steps and apply the power of God's Word and meditations to your life, you will begin the journey toward living the life you were born to live. No matter where you are or what challenges you face, *you can live at your full potential right now—and for the rest of your life!*

ENLARGE

YOUR VISION

We serve the Most High God,

and His dream for your life

is so much bigger and better

than you can even imagine.

LORD, I DRAW NEAR TO HEAR YOUR WORD

"For I know the plans I have for you," declares the LORD, *"plans to prosper you and not to harm you, plans to give you hope and a future."*

JEREMIAH 29:11

"FOR I AM ABOUT TO DO A BRAND-NEW THING. SEE, I HAVE ALREADY BEGUN! DO YOU NOT SEE IT? I WILL MAKE A PATHWAY THROUGH THE WILDERNESS FOR MY PEOPLE TO COME HOME. I WILL CREATE RIVERS FOR THEM IN THE DESERT!"

ISAIAH 43:19 NLT

Start Believing for More

We serve the God who created the universe. Never settle for a small view of God. He wants to do big things and new things in our lives. God wants us to be constantly increasing, to be rising to new heights. He wants to increase you in wisdom and help you make better decisions. He wants to increase you financially, by giving you promotions, fresh ideas, and creativity. He wants to pour out "His far and beyond favor" (Eph. 2:7).

Yet, it's interesting that God asks the question, "Do you not perceive it?" In other words, are you making room for it in your thinking?

It's time to *enlarge your vision*. To live your best life now, you must start looking at life through eyes of faith, seeing yourself rising to new levels. See your business taking off. See your marriage restored. See your family prospering. You must conceive it and believe it is possible if you ever hope to experience it.

Friend, if you will get in agreement with God, this can be the greatest time of your life. With God on your side, you cannot possibly lose. He can make a way when it looks as though there is no way. He can open doors that no man can shut. He can supernaturally turn your life around.

Get rid of small-minded thinking and start thinking as God thinks. Think big. Think increase. Think abundance. Think more than enough!

Your own wrong thinking
can keep you from God's best.

Making mention of you in my prayers…that you may know what is the hope of His calling, what are the riches of the glory of His inheritance in the saints, and what is the exceeding greatness of His power toward us who believe.

Ephesians 1:18–19

"Neither do men pour new wine into old wineskins. If they do, the skins will burst, the wine will run out and the wineskins will be ruined. No, they pour new wine into new wineskins, and both are preserved."

MATTHEW 9:17

Change Your Thinking

The good news is that it's not a lack of resources on God's part or His unwillingness to show you His incredible favor that prevents you from prospering. All too often the problem lies within. You may have assumed that you've reached your limits in life, that you will never be more successful or do something meaningful or enjoy the good things in life that you've seen others enjoy.

Sad to say, you are exactly right . . . unless you are willing to change your thinking and start believing for something bigger. Interestingly, when Jesus wanted to encourage His followers to enlarge their visions, He reminded them, "You can't put new wine into old wineskins." He was saying that you cannot have a larger life with restricted attitudes. Will you stretch your faith and vision and get rid of those old negative mind-sets that hold you back?

You don't have to be bound by the barriers of the past. Start making room in your thinking for what God has in store for you. You must conceive it in your heart and mind before you can receive it. The key is to believe, to let the seeds God is placing in your life to take root so they can grow. Expect God's favor to help you break out of the ruts and rise to new heights. Expect to excel in whatever you do.

Remember: With God, all things are possible.

Get beyond the barriers of the past and expect God to do great things in your life.

"Everything is possible for him who believes."

Mark 9:23

"It shall be done to you according to your faith."

With God on Your Side

God is constantly trying to plant new seeds in your heart. He's constantly trying to get you to conceive, to give up antiquated ideas, and spawn new bursts of creativity within. He's trying to fill you with so much hope and expectancy that the seed will grow and bring forth a tremendous harvest.

This is your time for increase. You may have been sick for a long time, but this is your time to get well. You may be bound by addictions and bad habits, but this is the time to be set free. You may be struggling financially, but this is the time for promotion. The key is to believe, to let the seed take root so it can grow.

God is saying to you something similar to what the angel told the Virgin Mary—that she would conceive without knowing a man. In other words, God was saying it would happen through supernatural means. What He wants to do in your life is not going to be by your might or power. It's going to be by His Spirit. The power of the Most High God shall come upon you and cause it to happen.

Will you allow that seed to take root? It can happen without a bank loan or having the right education. It can happen in spite of your past and what the critics are telling you. Will you believe?

With God, all things are possible.

Eliminate a barely-get-by mentality and let God's seed take root.

LORD, I DRAW NEAR TO HEAR YOUR WORD

SET YOUR MINDS AND KEEP THEM SET ON WHAT IS ABOVE (THE HIGHER THINGS), NOT ON THE THINGS THAT ARE ON THE EARTH.

COLOSSIANS 3:2 AMP

Faith is being sure of what we hope for and certain of what we do not see.

HEBREWS 11:1

Raise Your Level of Expectancy

God is extremely interested in what you see through your "spiritual eyes." If you have a vision for victory in your life, you can rise to a new level. But as long as your gaze is on the ground instead of on your possibilities, you risk moving in the wrong direction and missing out on the great things God wants to do in and through you. It's a spiritual as well as a psychological fact: We move toward what we see in our minds.

Your life will follow your *expectations*. What you expect is what you will get. If you dwell on positive thoughts, your life will move that direction; if you continually think negative thoughts, you will live a negative life. If you expect defeat, failure, or mediocrity, your subconscious mind will make sure that you lose, fail, or sabotage every attempt to push above average. If you raise your level of expectancy, you will enlarge your vision.

It's important that you program your mind for success. You must think positive thoughts of victory, of abundance, of favor, of hope. Each day, you must choose to live with an attitude that expects good things to happen to you. Start your day with faith and set your mind in the right direction, then go out expecting the favor of God. Expect to excel in your career and rise above life's challenges. Believe God for a great future. You have good things coming!

This could be the day you see your miracle.

Brethren, I do not count myself to have apprehended; but one thing I do, forgetting those things which are behind and reaching forward to those things which are ahead, I press toward the goal for the prize of the upward call of God in Christ Jesus. —PHILIPPIANS 3:13–14 NKJV

Stop Limiting God

God has more in store for you! His dream for your life is so much greater than you can imagine. If God showed you everything He has in store for you, it would boggle your mind.

It's time to quit limiting God. Remember: God is your source, and His creativity and resources are unlimited! God may give you an idea for an invention, a book, a song, or a movie. God can give you a dream. One idea from God can forever change the course of your life. God is not limited by what you have or don't have. God can do anything, if you will simply stop limiting Him in your thinking.

Maybe you hail from a long line of divorce, failure, depression, mediocrity, and other personal or family problems. You need to say, "Enough is enough. I'm going to break out of this cycle and change my expectations. I'm going to start believing God for bigger and better things."

When God puts a dream in your heart, when He brings opportunities across your path, step out boldly in faith, expect the best, move forward with confidence, knowing that you are well able to do what God wants you to do. God wants to do a new thing in your life. But you've got to do your part and get outside that little box you've grown accustomed to. Start thinking big!

What you will receive is directly connected to how you believe.

Enlarge the place of your tent, and let the curtains of your habitations be stretched out; spare not; lengthen your cords and strengthen your stakes, for you will spread abroad to the right hand and to the left.

ISAIAH 54:2–3 AMP

You have dwelt long enough on this mountain. . . . Behold, I have set the land before you; go in and take possession of the land which the Lord swore to your fathers, to Abraham, to Isaac, and to Jacob, to give to them and to their descendants after them.

DEUTERONOMY 1:6, 8 AMP

Break Through the Barriers

When God led the Hebrew people out of slavery in Egypt, the eleven-day journey to the Promised Land took forty years. God wanted them to move forward, but they wandered in the desert, going around the same mountain, time after time. They were trapped in a poor, defeated mentality, focusing on their problems, always complaining, and fretting about the obstacles between them and their destiny.

No matter what you've gone through in the past, no matter how many setbacks you've suffered or who or what has tried to thwart your progress, today is a new day, and God wants to do a new thing in your life. Don't let your past determine your future.

The Bible promises that "instead of your [former] shame" God will give us "a twofold recompense" (Isa. 61:7 AMP). That means if you'll keep the right attitude, God will pay you back double for your trouble. He'll add up all the injustices, all the pain and abuse that people have caused you, and He'll pay you back with twice as much joy, peace, and happiness. But you must do your part and start expecting good things.

You were born to win; you were born for greatness; you created to be a champion in life. Our God is called *El Shaddai*, "the God of more than enough." He's not "El Cheapo," the God of barely enough!

If you will change your thinking, God can change your life.

And we know that in
all things God works for
the good of those who
love him.

ROMANS 8:28

*Set your hope wholly
and unchangeably
on the grace
(divine favor)
that is coming
to you.*

1 PETER 1:13 AMP

God Will Open Doors for You

The Bible clearly states that God has crowned us with "glory and honor" (Psalm 8:5). The word *honor* could also be translated as "favor," and *favor* means "to assist, to provide with special advantages and to receive preferential treatment." In other words, God wants to assist you, to promote you, to give you advantages. But to experience more of God's favor, we must live more "favor-minded." We must expect God's special help and release our faith, knowing that God wants to assist us.

We can expect preferential treatment, not because of *who* we are, but because of *whose* we are. It is not because we are better than anybody else or that we deserve it. It is because our Father is the King of kings, and His glory and honor spill over onto us. As God's children we can live with confidence and boldness, expecting good things. If we love God, He's working life to our advantage, and it will all work out for our good, although it may not always be the way we hope. No matter what does or doesn't happen, keep believing for the favor of God.

Live favor-minded. Get up each day and expect and declare it. Say, "I have the favor of God." Don't sit back passively. You do your part, and God will do His part.

DON'T TAKE GOD'S FAVOR FOR GRANTED.

SURELY GOODNESS AND MERCY SHALL FOLLOW ME ALL THE DAYS OF MY LIFE.

PSALM 23:6 NKJV

*Your beauty
and love chase after
me every day of my life.*

PSALM 23:6 THE MESSAGE

The Power of an Attitude of Faith

When you are living favor-minded, the Bible says, "God's blessings are going to chase you down and overtake you." In other words, you won't be able to outrun the good things of God. Everywhere you go, things are going to change in your favor. Every time you turn around, somebody's going to want to do something good for you. It's all due to the favor of God.

The Bible is replete with examples of people who were in great need, but then the favor of God changed their situations. With the whole earth about to be destroyed by a flood, Noah "found favor" in the sight of God (Gen. 6:8) and built an ark to save his family, the animals, and himself. Practically starving to death, Ruth found "favor" with the owner of the grain field (Ruth 2:10), and eventually she and Naomi's dire circumstances turned around, and their needs were supplied in abundance. Despite overwhelming adversity in slavery in Egypt, the "favor" of God was upon Joseph (Gen. 39:5, 21, 23), and no matter what people did to him, he continued to thrive.

The favor of God comes in the midst of life's challenges. When you are going through tough times, even if your situation looks impossible, stay in an attitude of faith, and start declaring God's favor instead of being discouraged and developing a sour attitude. One touch of God's favor can turn everything around in your life.

Nothing is going to be able to keep you down.

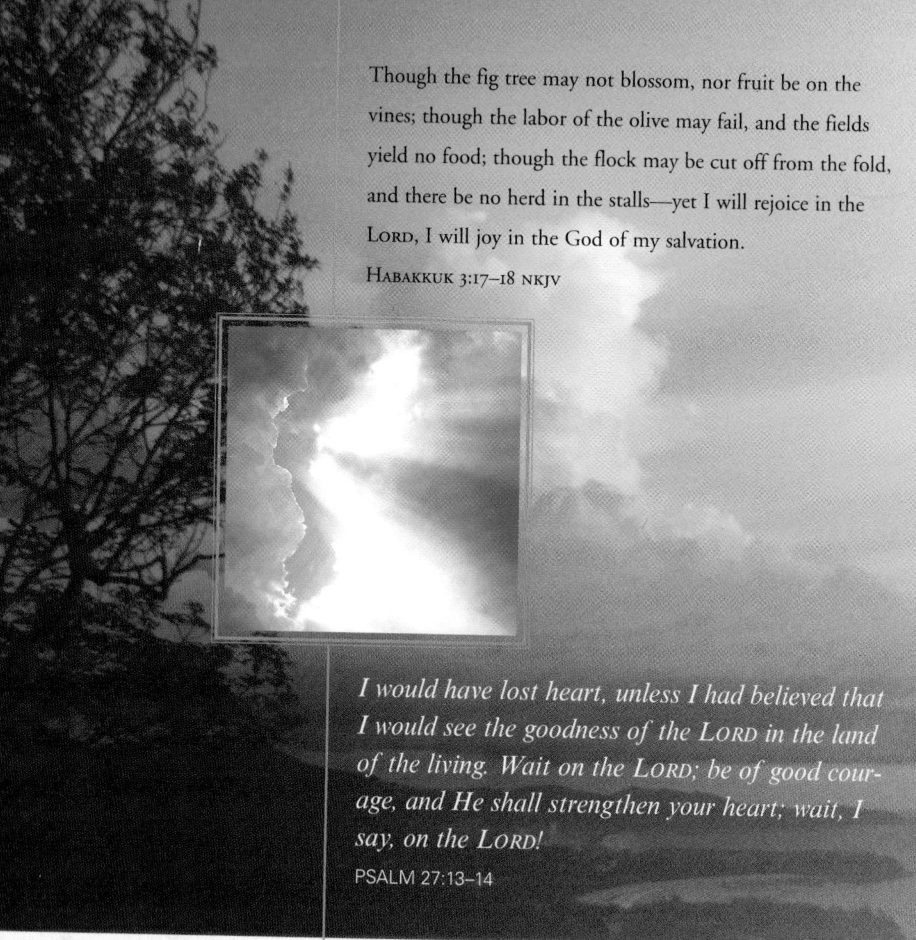

Though the fig tree may not blossom, nor fruit be on the vines; though the labor of the olive may fail, and the fields yield no food; though the flock may be cut off from the fold, and there be no herd in the stalls—yet I will rejoice in the LORD, I will joy in the God of my salvation.

HABAKKUK 3:17–18 NKJV

I would have lost heart, unless I had believed that I would see the goodness of the LORD in the land of the living. Wait on the LORD; be of good courage, and He shall strengthen your heart; wait, I say, on the LORD!

PSALM 27:13–14

NEVER RULE OUT GOD'S FAVOR

Is somebody mistreating you today? Are you struggling financially?

If you will live with an attitude of faith, before long God's favor is going to show up, and that difficult situation will turn around to your benefit. The Old Testament character Job went through one of the most trying times any person could ever endure. In less than a year, he lost his family, his business, and his health. He had boils over his entire body and no doubt lived in perpetual pain. But in the midst of that dark hour, Job said to God, "You have granted me life and favor" (Job 12:10 NKJV).

Now, here's the amazing part of the story: There are forty-two chapters in the book of Job. Job made this statement of faith in chapter 10. He was not delivered, healed, and set free until chapter 42! But at the very beginning, when his circumstances appeared darkest and most helpless, Job was saying, "God, I don't care what the situation looks like or how badly I feel. You are a good God. Your favor is going to turn this situation around."

No wonder God restored to Job twice what he had before! Friend, you may be in a situation today that looks impossible, but never rule out the favor of God. If you learn to stay in an attitude of faith and declare the favor of God, God promises that good things will come to you.

NEVER GIVE UP ON GOD.

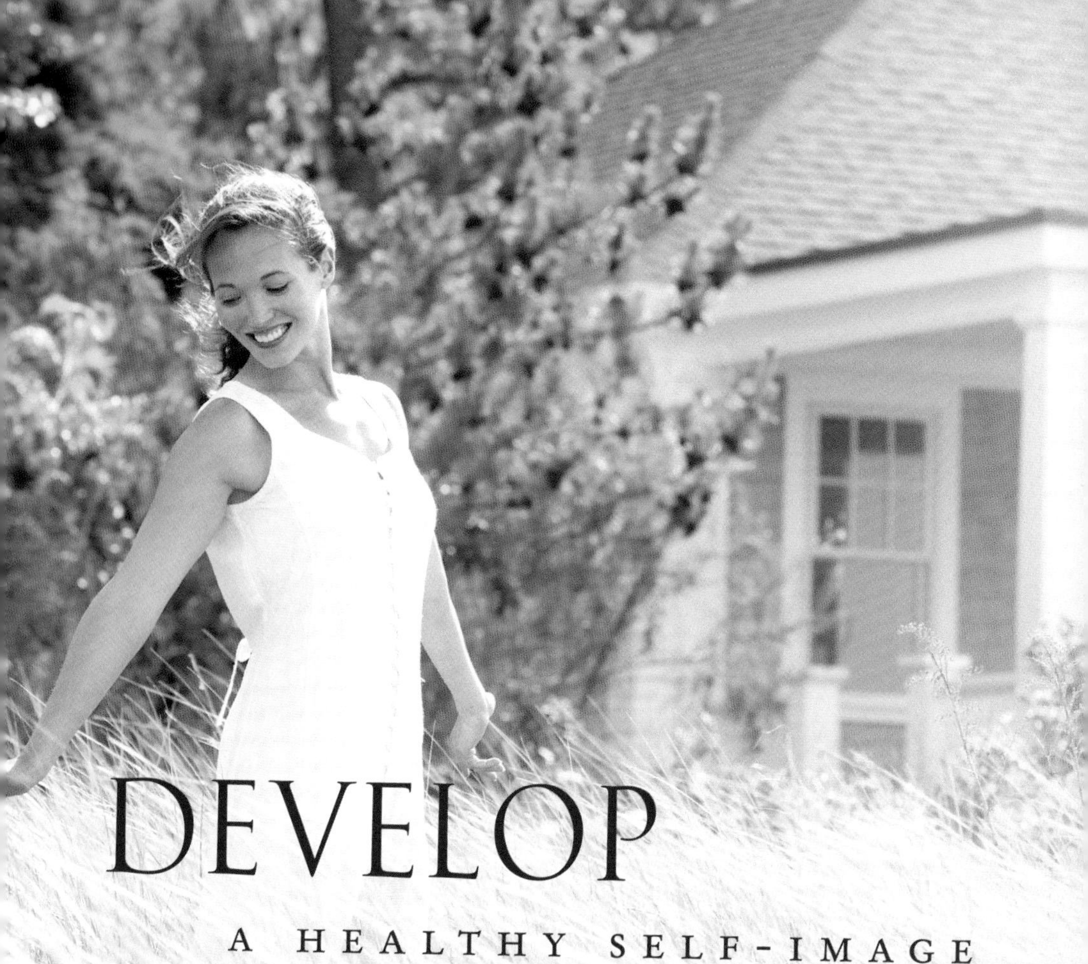

DEVELOP

A HEALTHY SELF-IMAGE

True self-esteem can be based

only on what God says about me—

not on what I think or feel

about myself.

I am who God says I am.

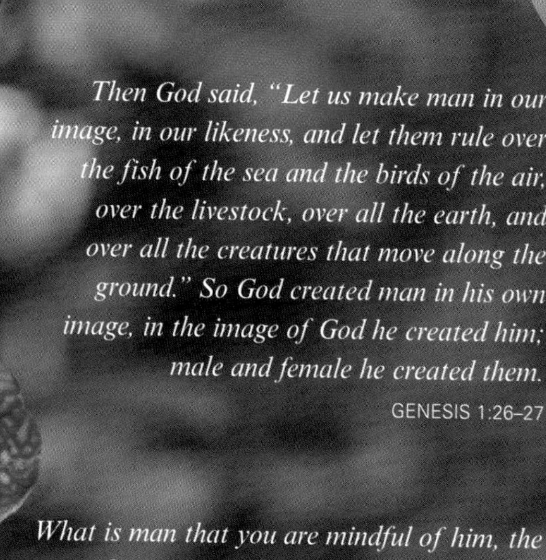

Then God said, "Let us make man in our image, in our likeness, and let them rule over the fish of the sea and the birds of the air, over the livestock, over all the earth, and over all the creatures that move along the ground." So God created man in his own image, in the image of God he created him; male and female he created them.

GENESIS 1:26–27

What is man that you are mindful of him, the son of man that you care for him? You made him a little lower than the heavenly beings and crowned him with glory and honor.

PSALM 8:4–5

Created in God's Image

Your self-image is much like a self-portrait; it is who and what you picture yourself to be, which may or may not be an accurate reflection of who you really are. How you feel about yourself will have a tremendous impact on how far you go in life, because you will probably speak, act, and react as the person you *think* you are. The truth is, you will never rise above the image you have of yourself in your mind.

God wants us to have healthy, positive self-images, to see ourselves as priceless treasures. He wants us to feel good about ourselves. Despite our faults and weaknesses, God loves us anyway. He created us in His image, and He is continually shaping us, conforming us to His character, helping us to become even more like the person He is. Consequently, we must learn to love ourselves, faults and all, not because we are egotists, but because that's how our heavenly Father loves us. You can walk with confidence knowing that God loves you unconditionally. His love for you is based on what you are, not what you do. He created you as a unique individual—there has never been, nor will there ever be, another person exactly like you, and He sees you as His special masterpiece!

You were made in the image of God.

God Sees You as a Champion

When the angel of the Lord appeared to tell Gideon how God wanted him to save the people of Israel from the Midianites, the first words spoken were, "The Lord is with you, you mighty man of [fearless] courage" (Judges 6:12 AMP). Gideon showed his true colors when he replied, "But Lord, how can I save Israel? My clan is the weakest in Manasseh, and I am the least in my family" (v. 15).

Sound familiar? So often, we sense God telling us that He has something big for us to do. But because of a poor self-image, we say, "God, I can't do that. You've got to find somebody more qualified. I don't have what it takes."

It's interesting to note the difference between the way Gideon saw himself and the way God rewarded him. Although Gideon felt unqualified, full of fear, and lacking in confidence, God addressed him as a mighty man of fearless courage. Gideon felt weak; God saw him as strong and competent to lead His people into battle and victory. And Gideon did!

Moreover, God sees you as a champion. He believes in you and regards you as a strong, courageous, successful, overcoming person. You may not see yourself that way, but that doesn't change God's image of you. God still sees you exactly as His Word describes you. You may feel unqualified, insecure, weak, fearful, and insignificant, but God sees you as a victor!

LEARN TO LOVE YOURSELF AS YOUR HEAVENLY FATHER LOVES YOU.

"The Lord is with you, you mighty man of valor!"

Judges 6:12 NKJV

But he said to me, "My grace is sufficient for you, for my power is made perfect in weakness." Therefore I will boast all the more gladly about my weaknesses, so that Christ's power may rest on me.

2 CORINTHIANS 12:9

Now thanks be to God who always leads us in triumph in Christ, and through us diffuses the fragrance of His knowledge in every place.

2 Corinthians 2:14 nkjv

But the path of the righteous is like the light of dawn, that shines brighter and brighter until the full day.

Proverbs 4:18 nasb

God loves to use ordinary people just like you and me, faults and all, to do extraordinary things. My question to you is: Are you allowing your weaknesses and insecurities to keep you from being your best? Are you letting feelings of inadequacy keep you from believing God for bigger things? God wants to use you in spite of your weaknesses. Don't focus on your weaknesses; focus on your God.

You may not feel capable in your own strength, but that's okay. The apostle Paul said, "When I am weak, then I am strong" (2 Cor. 12:10). God's Word states that He always causes us to triumph. He expects us to live victoriously. He is not pleased when we mope around with a "poor me" attitude. When you do that, you're allowing your self-image to be shaped by nonbiblical concepts that are contrary to God's opinions of you. This sort of poor self-image will keep you from exercising your God-given gifts and authority, and it will rob you from experiencing the abundant life your heavenly Father wants you to have.

You can change the image you have of yourself. Start by agreeing with God. Remember, God sees you as strong and courageous, as a man or woman of great honor and valor. He sees you as being more than a conqueror. Start seeing yourself as God sees you. Quit making excuses and start stepping out in faith, doing what God has called you to do.

God has already approved and accepted you.

"If the LORD is pleased with us, he will lead us into that land, a land flowing with milk and honey, and will give it to us. Only do not rebel against the LORD. And do not be afraid of the people of the land, because we will swallow them up. Their protection is gone, but the LORD is with us. Do not be afraid of them."

NUMBERS 14:8–9

IF GOD IS FOR US, WHO CAN BE AGAINST US?

ROMANS 8:31

Be a "Can Be" Person

Ten of the twelve Hebrew spies sent by Moses into Canaan to check out the opposition came back and said, "It is a land flowing with milk and honey, but there are giants in the land. Moses, we were in our own sight as grasshoppers. They're too strong. We'll never defeat them" (Num. 13). Compared to the giants, the mental image they had of themselves was as small, helpless grasshoppers. The battle was lost before it started.

Joshua and Caleb had a totally different report. "Moses, we are well able to possess the land. Yes, there are giants there, but our God is much bigger. Because of Him, we are well able. Let's go in at once and possess the land." Faced with the same giants, Joshua and Caleb believed God and refused to see themselves as grasshoppers. Instead, they saw themselves as God's men, led and empowered by God.

What a tremendous truth! You and I are "well able" people. Not because we are so powerful, but because our God is so powerful. Friend, God already has enough "grasshoppers." He wants you to be a "can do" person, someone who is willing, ready, and "well able" to do what He commands. You must learn how to cast down those negative thoughts and begin to see yourself as God sees you. You must reprogram your mind with God's Word; change that negative, defeated self-image, and start seeing yourself as winning.

Keep going; keep growing. God has much more in store for you!

You Are a Child of the Most High God

An important factor in seeing yourself God's way is to understand your intrinsic sense of value. Your sense of value cannot be based on your successes or failures, how somebody else treats you, or how popular you are. It is not something we earn; indeed, we cannot earn it. God built value into us when He created us. As His unique creation, you have something to offer this world that nobody else has, that nobody else can be. Your sense of value should be based solely on the fact that you are a child of the Most High God.

The Scripture says "we are God's workmanship" (Eph. 2:10). The word *workmanship* implies that you are a "work in progress." Throughout our lives, God is continually shaping us into the people He wants us to be. The key to future success is to not be discouraged about your past or present while you are in the process of being "completed."

God knows your value and loves you unconditionally. He sees your potential. You may not understand everything you are going through right now. But hold your head high, knowing that God is in control and He has a great plan and purpose for your life. Your dreams may not have turned out exactly as you'd hoped, but the Bible says that God's ways are better and higher than our ways. Even if everybody else rejects you, remember, God stands before you with His arms open wide.

Learn to be happy with who God made you to be.

And I am convinced and sure of this very thing, that He Who began a good work in you will continue until the day of Jesus Christ [right up to the time of His return], developing [that good work] and perfecting and bringing it to full completion in you.

PHILIPPIANS 1:6 AMP

BUT WE ALL, WITH OPEN FACE BEHOLDING AS IN A GLASS THE GLORY OF THE LORD, ARE CHANGED INTO THE SAME IMAGE FROM GLORY TO GLORY, EVEN AS BY THE SPIRIT OF THE LORD.

2 CORINTHIANS 3:18 KJV

[God said to Abraham,] "I will bless you and make your name famous, and you will be a blessing to many others."

GENESIS 12:2 TLB

Become What You Believe

In the New Testament, there is a fascinating account of two blind men who heard that Jesus was passing by, and faith began to rise in their hearts. They must have thought, *We don't have to stay like this. There's hope for a better future.* So they began to cry out, "Have mercy on us, Son of David!" (Matt. 9:27).

When Jesus heard their cries, He posed an intriguing question, "'Do you believe that I am able to do this?'" (v. 28 NASB). Jesus wanted to know whether they had genuine faith. The blind men answered, "Yes, Lord; we believe." The Bible says, "Then He touched their eyes, saying, According to your faith and trust and reliance [on the power invested in Me] be it done to you; and their eyes were opened" (v. 29–30 AMP).

Notice, it was their faith that brought them the healing. *The Message* says, "[Jesus] touched their eyes and said, 'Become what you believe.'" What a powerful statement! Become what you believe! What are you believing? Are you believing to go higher in life, to rise above your obstacles, to live in health, abundance, healing, and victory? You will become what you believe.

You don't have to figure out how God is going to solve your problems or bring it to pass. That's His responsibility. Your job is to believe. What you believe has a much greater impact on your life than what anybody else believes.

YOUR FAITH WILL HELP YOU OVERCOME YOUR OBSTACLES.

Praise be to the God and Father of our Lord Jesus Christ, who has blessed us in the heavenly realms with every spiritual blessing in Christ.

EPHESIANS 1:3

"WELL DONE, GOOD AND FAITHFUL SERVANT; YOU WERE FAITHFUL OVER A FEW THINGS, I WILL MAKE YOU RULER OVER MANY THINGS. ENTER INTO THE JOY OF YOUR LORD."

MATTHEW 25:21 NKJV

Look Through Eyes of Faith

One of the most important aspects of seeing ourselves God's way involves developing a prosperous mind-set. Understand, God has already equipped you with everything you need to live a prosperous life and to fulfill your God-given destiny. He planted "seeds" inside you filled with possibilities, incredible potential, creative ideas, and dreams. But you have to start tapping into them. You've got to believe beyond a shadow of a doubt that you have what it takes. God created you to excel, and He's given you ability, insight, talent, wisdom, and His supernatural power to do so.

For instance, the Bible says, "We are more than conquerors through him who loved us" (Rom. 8:37). It doesn't say we will become conquerors; it says we are more than conquerors *right now*. If you will start acting like it, talking like it, seeing yourself as more than a conqueror, you will live a prosperous and victorious life. The price has already been paid for you to have joy, peace, and happiness. That's part of the package that God has made available to you.

Start looking through eyes of faith, seeing yourself rising to new levels. See yourself prospering, and keep that image in your heart and mind. You may be living in poverty at the moment, but don't ever let poverty live in you. The Bible shows that God takes pleasure in prospering His children. As His children prosper spiritually, physically, and materially, their increase brings God pleasure.

God has everything you need.

Be the Original You

Dare to be happy with who you are right now. Many social, physical, and emotional problems stem from the fact that people don't like themselves. They are uncomfortable with how they look, how they talk, or how they act. They don't like their personality. They are always comparing themselves with other people, wishing they were something different.

You were not created to mimic somebody else. You were created to be you. You can be happy with who God made you to be, and quit wishing you were something different. If God had wanted you to look like anyone else, He would have made you look like them. If God had wanted you to have a different personality, He would have given you that personality. When you go around trying to be like somebody else, not only does it demean you, it steals your uniqueness.

God doesn't want a bunch of clones. He likes variety, and you should not let people pressure you or make you feel badly about yourself because you don't fit their image of who you should be. Be an original, not a copycat. Dare to be different; be secure in who God made you to be and then go out and be the best you that you can be. You don't need anybody else's approval. God has given us all different gifts, talents, and personalities on purpose. Learn to be happy with who God made you.

If you run the race and be the best that you can be, then you can feel good about yourself.

Each one should test his own actions. Then he can take pride in himself, without comparing himself to somebody else, for each one should carry his own load.

Galatians 6:4–5

I know the Lord is always with me. I will not be shaken, for he is right beside me.

Psalm 16:8 NLT

DISCOVER
THE POWER OF YOUR
THOUGHTS AND WORDS

Keep your mind set on the reality

that God is a miracle-working God.

Start talking to your mountains

about how big your God is!

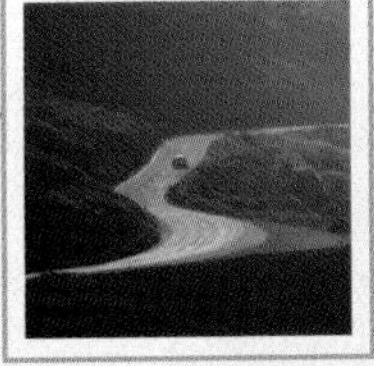

Success Begins in the Mind

The third step to living at your full potential is to discover the power of your thoughts and words. Whether or not you are aware of it, a war is raging all around you, and the battle is for your mind. Your enemy's number one target is the arena of your thoughts. If he can control how you think, he'll be able to control your entire life. Indeed, thoughts determine actions, attitudes, and self-image. Really, thoughts determine destiny, which is why the Bible warns us to guard our minds.

Almost like a magnet, we draw in what we constantly think about. If we dwell on depressing, negative thoughts, we will be depressed and negative. If we think positive, happy, joyful thoughts, our life will reflect that and attract other upbeat, positive people. Our life follows our thoughts.

And our thoughts also affect our emotions. We will feel exactly the way we think. You cannot expect to feel happy unless you think happy thoughts. Conversely, it's impossible to remain discouraged unless you first think discouraging thoughts. So much of success and failure in life begins in our minds.

Set your mind on the right course. Start every day by agreeing with the psalmist, "This is the day the Lord has made, and I'm going to be happy. I'm going to go out and be productive. This is going to be a great day." Magnify your God, and go out each day expecting good things.

Every day, when you first get up, set your mind for success.

"This is what the Lord says to you:
'Do not be afraid or discouraged because of this vast army. For the battle is not yours, but God's.' "

2 Chronicles 20:15

You will keep in perfect peace him whose mind is steadfast, because he trusts in you.

Isaiah 26:3

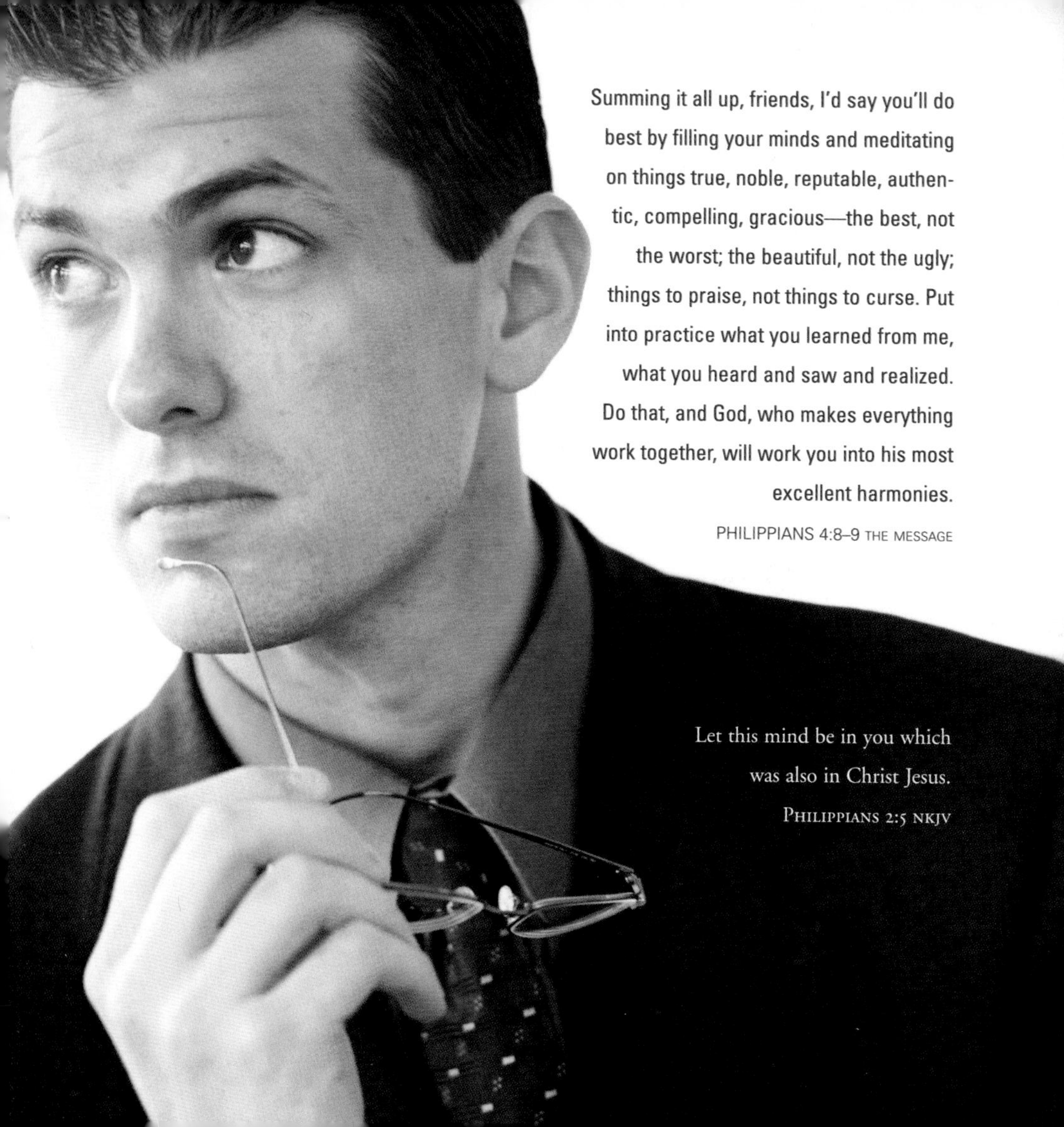

Summing it all up, friends, I'd say you'll do best by filling your minds and meditating on things true, noble, reputable, authentic, compelling, gracious—the best, not the worst; the beautiful, not the ugly; things to praise, not things to curse. Put into practice what you learned from me, what you heard and saw and realized. Do that, and God, who makes everything work together, will work you into his most excellent harmonies.

PHILIPPIANS 4:8–9 THE MESSAGE

Let this mind be in you which was also in Christ Jesus.

PHILIPPIANS 2:5 NKJV

Think About Your Thinking

Life is tough. We all get knocked down occasionally and get discouraged, but we need not remain there. We can choose our thoughts. Nobody can make us think a certain way. If you're not happy, nobody is forcing you to be unhappy. If you're negative and have a bad attitude, nobody's coercing you to be sarcastic or sullen. You decide what you will entertain in your mind.

Simply because the enemy plants a negative, discouraging thought in your brain doesn't mean you have to nurture and help it grow. If you do, though, that thought will affect your emotions, your attitudes, and eventually your actions. You will be much more prone to discouragement and depression, and if you continue pondering that negative thought, it will sap the energy and strength right out of you.

We must take responsibility for our minds and our actions. As long as we keep making excuses and blaming the family tree, our environment, past relationships with other people, our circumstances, and attributing blame to God, Satan, anyone, or anything, we will never be truly free and emotionally healthy. To a large extent, we can control our own destinies.

It's not your circumstances that have you down; your thoughts about your circumstances have you down. It is possible to be in one of the biggest battles for your life and still be filled with joy and peace and victory—if you simply learn how to choose the right thoughts.

We can choose to believe that God is greater than our problems.

As You Think, You Will Be

It is unrealistic to pretend that nothing bad ever happens to us. Bad things happen to good people. Pretense is not the answer; nor is playing semantic games to make yourself sound more spiritual. If you are sick, admit it; but keep your thoughts on your Healer. If your body is tired, if your spirit is weary, fine: but focus your thoughts on the One who has promised, "Those who wait on the Lord shall renew their strength" (Isa. 40:31 NKJV).

Jesus said, "In the world you will have tribulation; but be of good cheer, I have overcome the world" (John 16:33 NKJV). He wasn't saying that troublesome times wouldn't come; He was saying that when they do, we can choose our attitudes. We can choose to believe that He is greater than our problems.

The first place we must win the victory is in our own minds. You can't sit back passively and expect this new person to suddenly appear. If you don't think you can be successful, you never will be. If you don't think your body can be healed, it never will be. When you think thoughts of mediocrity, you are destined to live an average life. But when you align your thoughts with God's thoughts and you start dwelling on the promises of His Word, when you constantly dwell on thoughts of His victory and favor, you will be propelled toward greatness, inevitably bound for increase, promotion, and God's supernatural blessings.

Choose to dwell on the promises of God's Word.

Do not be anxious about anything, but in everything, by prayer and petition, with thanksgiving, present your requests to God. And the peace of God, which transcends all understanding, will guard your hearts and your minds in Christ Jesus.

Philippians 4:6–7

As he thinks within himself, so he is.

Proverbs 23:7 NASB

We demolish arguments and every pretension that sets itself up against the knowledge of God, and we take captive every thought to make it obedient to Christ.

2 Corinthians 10:5

Strip yourselves of your former nature . . . and be constantly renewed in the spirit of your mind [having a fresh mental and spiritual attitude].

Ephesians 4:22–23 AMP

Guard Your Mind

When the Bible says, "Set your minds on things above" (Col. 3:2), it means that we must continually choose, twenty-four hours a day, to keep our minds on the positive things of God. The apostle Paul provides a great list by which we can evaluate our thoughts: "whatever is pure, whatever is lovely and lovable, whatever is kind and winsome and gracious . . . if there is anything worthy of praise, think and weigh and take account of these things" (Phil. 4:8 AMP).

So how do you ascertain the source of a thought? Easy. If it's a discouraging, destructive thought; if it brings fear, worry, doubt, or unbelief; if the thought makes you feel weak, insecure, or inadequate, I can guarantee you that thought is not from God. You need to get rid of it immediately. If you dwell on the enemy's lies and the negative takes root, it creates an enemy stronghold in your mind from which attacks can be launched.

You must make a quality choice to keep your mind focused on the good things of God and experience His best for your life. We must be especially on guard during times of adversity, in times of personal challenge. When troubles strike, often the first thoughts that come to mind are not positive thoughts. Negative thoughts and fear bombard us from every possible angle. Right there, we must choose to trust God and know that He has great things in store for us.

I will stay focused and full of hope, knowing that God is fighting my battles for me.

There is a river whose streams make glad the city of God, the holy dwelling places of the Most High.

Psalm 46:4 NASB

"I have set before you life and death, blessing and cursing; therefore choose life, that both you and your descendants may live."

Deuteronomy 30:19 NKJV

Transform Your Thinking

Let's be real. If your thoughts have been running in a negative pattern for month after month, year after year, it's as though they have been eroding a deep riverbed, and the negativity can flow in only one direction. With every pessimistic thought, the riverbed is a bit deeper and the current stronger. It is possible to program your mind into a negative thinking pattern.

Fortunately, we can cause a new river to flow, one going in a positive direction. When you dwell on God's Word and start seeing the best in situations, little by little, one thought at a time, you are redirecting the flow of that river. It may not look like much at first, but as you continue to reject negative thoughts and redirect the flow, as you choose faith instead of fear, expecting good things and taking control of your thought life, that negative stream will dwindle and the positive river will flow with positive, faith-filled thoughts of victory.

Friend, don't sit back and allow negative, critical thoughts to influence your life. The Bible tells to be "transformed by the renewing of your mind" (Rom. 12:2). Keep in mind, though, that river of negativity wasn't formed overnight, nor will it be redirected without some conscious, strenuous effort on your part. God will help you. Stay full of faith. Stay full of joy. Stay full of hope. If you will transform your thinking, God will transform your life.

You have a new river flowing.

The Power of Your Words

Our words have tremendous power and are similar to seeds. By speaking them aloud, they are planted in our subconscious minds, take root, grow, and produce fruit of the same kind. Whether we speak positive or negative words, we will reap exactly what we sow. That's why we need to be extremely careful what we think and say.

The Bible compares the tongue to the rudder of a huge ship (James 3:4). Although the rudder is small, it controls the ship's direction. Similarly, your tongue will control the direction of your life. You create an environment for either good or evil with your words, and you are going to have to live in that world you've created. If you're always murmuring, complaining, and talking about how bad life is treating you, you're going to live in a pretty miserable world. However, God wants us to use our words to *change* our negative situations.

The Bible clearly tells us to speak to our mountains. Maybe your mountain is a sickness, or a troubled relationship, or a floundering business. Whatever your mountain is, you must do more than think about it, more than pray about it; you must speak to that obstacle. The Bible says, "Let the weak say, 'I am strong'" (Joel 3:10). Start calling yourself healed, happy, whole, blessed, and prosperous. Stop talking to God about how big your mountains are, and starting talking to your mountains about how big your God is!

God is a miracle-working God.

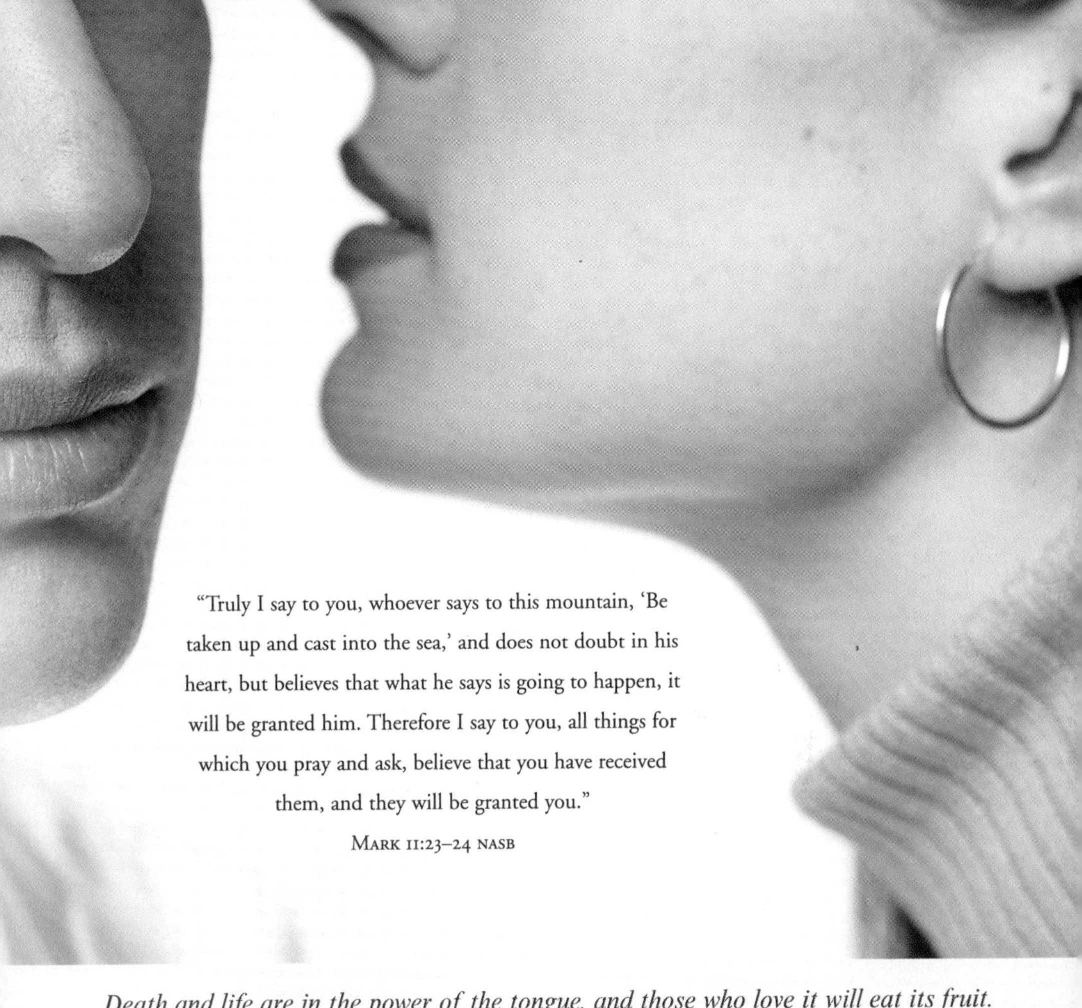

"Truly I say to you, whoever says to this mountain, 'Be taken up and cast into the sea,' and does not doubt in his heart, but believes that what he says is going to happen, it will be granted him. Therefore I say to you, all things for which you pray and ask, believe that you have received them, and they will be granted you."

MARK 11:23–24 NASB

Death and life are in the power of the tongue, and those who love it will eat its fruit.

PROVERBS 18:21 NASB

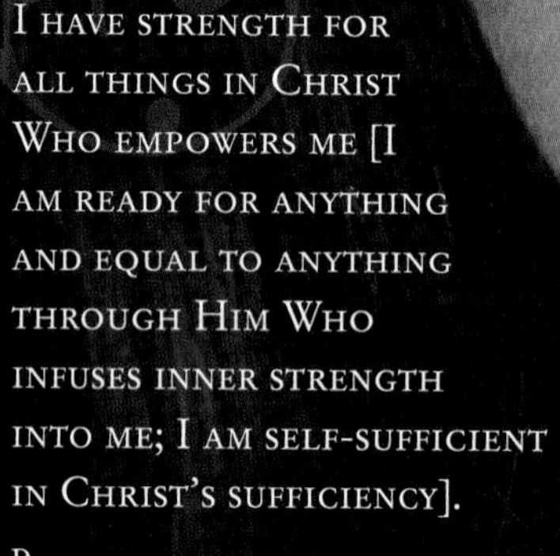

I have strength for all things in Christ Who empowers me [I am ready for anything and equal to anything through Him Who infuses inner strength into me; I am self-sufficient in Christ's sufficiency].

Philippians 4:13 AMP

For it is with your heart that you believe and are justified, and it is with your mouth that you confess and are saved. As the Scripture says, "Anyone who trusts in him will never be put to shame."

ROMANS 10:10–11

THE MIRACLE IN YOUR MOUTH

I love what David did when he faced the giant Goliath. He didn't complain and say, "God, why do I always have huge problems?" He didn't dwell on the fact that Goliath was three times his size or that Goliath was a skilled warrior and he was just a shepherd boy. Rather than focus on the magnitude of the obstacle before him, David chose to focus on the greatness of God.

David looked Goliath right in the eyes and changed his whole atmosphere through the words he spoke aloud. He said, "You come against me with sword and spear and javelin, but I come against you in the name of the LORD Almighty, the God of the armies of Israel, whom you have defied" (1 Sam. 17:45).

Now, those are words of faith! He didn't merely *think* them; he didn't simply *pray* them. He spoke directly to the mountain of a man in front of him and said, "Today I will give the carcasses of the Philistine army to the birds of the air" (v. 46). And with God's help, he did!

Friend, there is a miracle in your mouth. If you want to change your world, start by changing your words. When you're facing obstacles in your path, you must boldly say, "Greater is He who is in me than he who is in the world. No weapon formed against me is going to prosper. God always causes me to triumph."

USE YOUR WORDS TO CHANGE YOUR SITUATION.

"But the word is very near you, in your mouth and in your heart, that you may observe it."

DEUTERONOMY 30:14 NASB

Reckless words pierce like a sword, but the tongue of the wise brings healing.

PROVERBS 12:18

Speak Words of Faith

Our words are vital in bringing our dreams to pass. It's not enough to simply see it by faith or in your imagination. You have to begin speaking words of faith over your life. Your words have enormous creative power. The moment you speak something out, you give birth to it. This is a spiritual principle, and it works whether what you are saying is positive or negative.

In that regard, many times we are our own worst enemies. We blame everybody and everything else, but the truth is, we are profoundly influenced by what we say about ourselves. Scripture says, "You are snared by the words of your mouth" (Prov. 6:2 NKJV).

Statements such as, "Nothing good ever happens to me," will literally prevent you from moving ahead in life. That's why you must learn to guard your tongue and speak only faith-filled words over your life. This is one of the most important principles you can ever grab hold of. Simply put, your words can make or break you.

Understand, avoiding negative talk is not enough. You must start using your words to move forward in life. When you believe God's Word and begin to boldly confess it, mixing it with your faith, you are actually confirming that truth and making it valid in your own life. And all heaven comes to attention to back up God's Word, bringing to life the great things God has in store for you.

Speak words of victory, health, and success about your life.

A WORD APTLY SPOKEN IS LIKE APPLES OF GOLD IN SETTINGS OF SILVER.

PROVERBS 25:11

Out of the same mouth proceed blessing and cursing. My brethren, these things ought not to be so.

JAMES 3:10 NKJV

The Power of Blessing

Whether we realize it or not, our words affect our children's future for either good or evil. We need to speak loving words of approval and acceptance, words that encourage, inspire, and motivate our family members to reach for new heights. When we do that, we speak blessings into their lives, words that carry spiritual authority much like the Old Testament patriarch's blessing of his children (Gen. 27:1–41). We are speaking abundance and increase, declaring God's favor in their lives.

But too often, we are harsh and fault-finding with our children. Our negative words will cause our children to lose the sense of value God has placed within them and can allow the enemy to bring all kinds of insecurity and inferiority into their lives.

What are you passing down to the next generation? It's not enough to think it; you must vocalize it. A blessing is not a blessing until it is spoken. Your children need to hear you say words such as, "I love you. I believe in you. I think you're great. There's nobody else like you." They need to hear your approval. They need to feel your love. They need your blessing.

Use your words to speak blessing over people. Husbands, bless your wives with your words. You can help set the direction for your employees with your positive words. Learn to speak blessings over your friends. Start speaking those blessings today!

Speak words that encourage, inspire, and motivate.

LET GO

OF THE PAST

It's time to allow your emotional wounds to heal. Let go of your excuses, and stop feeling sorry for yourself. It's time to get rid of your victim mentality.

Through the LORD's mercies we are not consumed, because His compassions fail not. They are new every morning; great is Your faithfulness. —LAMENTATIONS 3:22–23 NKJV
"Come to me, all you who are weary and burdened, and I will give you rest."
MATTHEW 11:28

Letting Go

We live in a society that loves to make excuses, and one of our favorite phrases is: "It's not my fault." But the truth is, if we are bitter and resentful, it's because we are allowing ourselves to remain that way. We've all had negative things happen to us. If you look hard enough, anyone can make excuses and blame the past for his bad attitude, poor choices, or hot temper.

You may have valid reasons. You may have gone through things that nobody deserves to experience in life—physical, verbal, sexual, or emotional abuse. Maybe you've struggled with a chronic illness or an irreparable physical problem. Maybe your dreams didn't work out. I don't mean to minimize those difficult experiences, but if you want to live in victory, you can't let your past poison your future.

It's time to allow emotional wounds to heal, to let go of your excuses and stop feeling sorry for yourself. It's time to get rid of your victim mentality. Nobody—not even God—ever promised that life would be fair. Quit comparing your life to someone else's, and quit dwelling on what could or should have been. Quit asking questions such as, "Why this?" or "Why that?" or "Why me?" Let go of those hurts and pains. Forgive the people who did you wrong. Forgive yourself for the mistakes you've made.

Today can be a new beginning.

SHAKE OFF THE BAGGAGE

Friend, don't be a prisoner of the past. Some people are always dwelling on their disappointments. They can't understand why their prayers aren't being answered, why their loved one wasn't healed, why they were mistreated. Some people have lived so long in self-pity that it has become part of their identity. They don't realize that God wants to restore what's been stolen.

If you're not willing to let go of the old, don't expect God to do the new. If you've had some unfair things happen to you, make a decision that you're going to quit reliving those things in your memory. Instead, think on good things, things that will build you up and not tear you down, things that will encourage you and give you the hope that there's a brighter tomorrow.

Why? Because your life is going to follow your thoughts. If you're constantly dwelling on all the negative things that have happened to you, focused on the mistakes you've made and what you've done wrong, then you're perpetuating that problem. You will never be truly happy as long as you harbor bitterness in your heart.

You may even need to forgive God. Perhaps you've been blaming Him for taking one of your loved ones or because your situation didn't work out after you prayed about it. If you don't deal with it, you will wallow in self-pity. You must let go of those negative attitudes and the accompanying anger. Let it go.

IF YOU'RE GOING TO GO FORWARD IN LIFE, YOU MUST QUIT LOOKING BACKWARD.

"You will know the truth, and the truth will set you free."

John 8:32

You'll use the
old rubble of
past lives to build
anew, rebuild
the foundations
from out of your
past. You'll be known
as those who can fix
anything, restore old ruins,
rebuild and renovate, make
the community livable again.

Isaiah 58:12 The Message

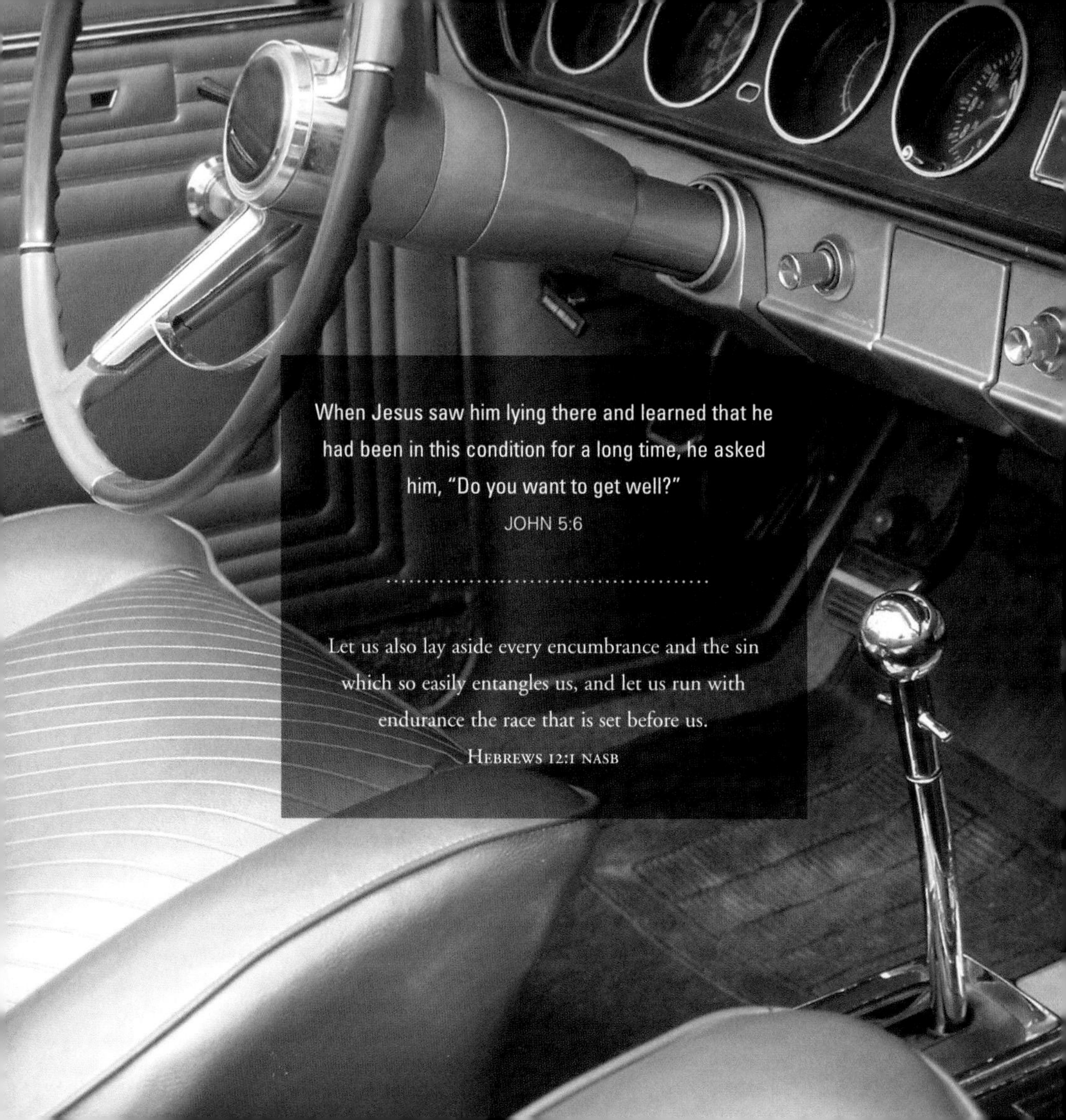

When Jesus saw him lying there and learned that he had been in this condition for a long time, he asked him, "Do you want to get well?"

JOHN 5:6

Let us also lay aside every encumbrance and the sin which so easily entangles us, and let us run with endurance the race that is set before us.

HEBREWS 12:1 NASB

Get Up and Get Movin'

A man in Jerusalem had been crippled for thirty-eight years. He spent every day of his life lying by the pool of Bethesda, hoping for a miracle (John 5). This man had a deep-seated, lingering disorder similar to what many people have today. Their maladies may not be physical; they may be emotional, but they are deep-seated, lingering disorders nonetheless. They may stem from unforgiveness or holding on to past resentments, and they affect your personality, your relationships, and your self-image. Just as the man lying by the pool, some people sit back for years, waiting for a miracle to happen that will make everything better.

When Jesus saw the man lying there, He asked a simple, straightforward question: "Do you want to be made well?" The man's response was interesting. He began listing all of his excuses. "I'm all alone. I don't have anyone to help me." Is it any wonder that he had not been healed?

Jesus looked at him and said, in effect, "If you are serious about getting well, if you want to get out of this mess, get up off the ground, take up your bed, and be on your way." When the man did what Jesus told him to do, he was miraculously healed!

If you're serious about being well, you can't lie around feeling sorry for yourself. Stop making excuses. Trust God, get up, and step into the great future He has for you.

Today can be a turning point in your life.

"Do not judge, and you will not be judged. Do not condemn, and you will not be condemned. Forgive, and you will be forgiven."

Luke 6:37

Make this your common practice: Confess your sins to each other and pray for each other so that you can live together whole and healed.

JAMES 5:16 THE MESSAGE

The "Why" Questions

King David prayed and fasted for seven days, nevertheless his newborn baby died (2 Sam. 12:1–25). Although David had been extremely distraught, he did not get bitter or question God. Instead, he dared to trust God in the midst of his disappointment. He washed his face and moved on with his life.

Don't waste another minute trying to figure out why certain evil things have happened to you or your loved ones. You may never know the answer. But don't use that as an excuse to wallow in self-pity. Leave it alone, get up, and move on with your life. Trust God and accept the fact that there will be some unanswered questions. Just because you don't know the answer doesn't mean that one does not exist.

Each of us should have what I call an "I Don't Understand It" file. When something comes up for which you have no reasonable answer, instead of dwelling on the "why," simply place it in this file and don't become bitter. You must walk out of any emotional bondage in which you have been living. Learn to do what David did: Just wash your face, keep a good attitude, and move on. If you will stay in an attitude of faith and victory, God has promised that He will turn those emotional wounds around. He'll use them to your advantage, and you will come out better than you would have had they not happened to you.

When you go through situations you don't understand, don't become bitter.

Bitterness Be Gone

A lot of people are trying to improve their lives by dealing with the external aspects. They are attempting to rectify their bad habits, bad attitudes, bad tempers, or negative and sour personalities. Trying to change the fruit of their lives is noble, but unless they get to the root, they will never change the fruit. As long as a bitter internal root is growing, the problems will persist. You may be able to control your behavior or keep a good attitude for a while, but you can't be free.

You have to go deeper. Many people attempt to bury the hurt and pain in their hearts or their subconscious minds. They don't realize it, but much of their inner turmoil is because their own heart is poisoned. The Bible says, "Keep thy heart with all diligence; for out of it are the issues of life" (Prov. 4:23 KJV). In other words, if we have bitterness on the inside, it's going to end up contaminating everything that comes out of us. It will contaminate our personalities and our attitudes, as well as how we treat other people.

If you are harboring anger, ask yourself why. If you have trouble getting along with other people, if you're always negative—about yourself, about others, about life in general—dare to ask yourself why this is. When you get to the root, you'll be able to deal with the problem, overcome it, and can truly begin to change.

Once the bitter root is gone, you will be able to break free from your past.

See to it that no one misses the grace of God and that no bitter root grows up to cause trouble and defile many.

HEBREWS 12:15

Forgive us our sins, just as we have forgiven those who have sinned against us.

Matthew 6:12/NLT

Be kind to one another, tender-hearted, forgiving each other, just as God in Christ also has forgiven you.

EPHESIANS 4:32 NASB

"FOR IF YOU FORGIVE MEN WHEN THEY SIN AGAINST YOU, YOUR HEAVENLY FATHER WILL ALSO FORGIVE YOU. BUT IF YOU DO NOT FORGIVE MEN THEIR SINS, YOUR FATHER WILL NOT FORGIVE YOUR SINS."

MATTHEW 6:14–15

Forgive to Be Free

If you want to live your best life now, you must be quick to forgive. You need to forgive so you can be free, out of bondage, and happy. When we forgive, we're not doing it just for the other person, we're doing it for our own good. When we hold on to unforgiveness and live with grudges in our hearts, all we're doing is building walls of separation. We think we're protecting ourselves, but we're not. We are simply shutting other people out of our lives. We become isolated, alone, warped, and imprisoned by our own bitterness. Those walls don't merely keep people out; those walls keep you penned in.

Do you realize that those walls will also prevent God's blessings from pouring into your life? Those walls can stop the flow of God's favor and keep your prayers from being answered. They'll keep your dreams from coming to pass. You must tear down the walls. You must forgive the people who hurt you so you can get out of prison. You'll never be free until you do. Let go of those wrongs they've done to you. Get that bitterness out of your life. That's the only way you're going to truly be free.

You may experience genuine physical and emotional healing as you search your heart and are willing to forgive. You may see God's favor in a fresh, new way. You'll be amazed at what can happen when you release all that poison.

FORGIVENESS IS A CHOICE, BUT IT IS NOT AN OPTION.

Doing Right When It Hurts

Being cheated in a business deal, betrayed by a friend, walked out on by a loved one—certainly, these kinds of losses leave indelible scars, causing you to want to hold on to your grief. It would be logical for you to seek revenge. Many people would even encourage you to do so. The slogan "Don't get mad, get even!" is a commonly accepted principle in America today.

But that is not God's plan for you. God has promised that if you will put your trust in Him to bring about the justice in your life, He will pay you back for all the unfair things that have happened to you (Isa. 61:7–9). That means you don't have to go around trying to pay everybody back for the wrong things they have done to you. God is your vindicator. Let Him fight your battles for you. Turn matters over to Him and let Him handle them His way.

When you truly understand that you don't have to fix everything that happens to you, you don't have to get all upset and try to get even with people for what they did or didn't do. You don't have to try to manipulate the situation or control the circumstances or people involved. When you leave it up to God to pay you back, you take the high road, respond in love, and watch what God will do. Remember, God always pays back abundantly.

God can turn your situation around and make it all up to you, plus much more!

For the LORD will vindicate His people, and will have compassion on His servants.
Deuteronomy 32:36 NASB

Beloved, never avenge yourselves, but leave the way open for [God's] wrath; for it is written, Vengeance is Mine, I will repay (requite), says the Lord.
Romans 12:19 AMP

The Lord is wonderfully good to those who wait for him and seek him.
Lamentations 3:25 NLT

"The Spirit of the Lord God is upon Me, because the Lord has anointed Me to preach good tidings to the poor; He has sent Me to heal the brokenhearted . . . to console those who mourn in Zion, to give them beauty for ashes, the oil of joy for mourning, the garment of praise for the spirit of heaviness."
Isaiah 61:1–3 NKJV

Keep Moving Forward

One of the most important keys to moving forward into the great future God has for you is learning how to overcome the disappointments in your life. Because disappointments can pose such formidable obstacles to letting go of the past, you need to be sure you have dealt with this area before taking the next step to living at your full potential.

Often, defeating disappointments and letting go of the past are the flip side of the same coin, especially when you are disappointed in yourself. When you do something wrong, don't hold on to it and beat yourself up about it. Admit it, seek forgiveness, and move on. Be quick to let go of your mistakes and failures, hurts, pains, and sins.

When you suffer loss, nobody expects you to be an impenetrable rock. When we experience failure or loss, it's natural to feel remorse or sorrow. That's the way God made us. But you must make a decision that you are going to move on. It won't happen automatically. You will have to rise up and say, "I don't care how hard this is, I am not going to let this get the best of me."

Don't live in regret or remorse or sorrow. They will only interfere with your faith. Faith must always be a present-tense reality, not a distant memory. God will turn those disappointments around. He will take your scars and turn them into stars for His glory.

Don't let your setbacks become your identity.

FIND
STRENGTH
THROUGH
ADVERSITY

God has a divine purpose

for every challenge

that comes into our lives.

Trials test our character

and help shape our faith.

Use every piece of God's armor to resist the enemy in the time of evil, so that after the battle you will still be standing firm.

Ephesians 6:13 NLT

Get Up on the Inside

Living your best life now is downright difficult sometimes. Many people give up far too easily when things don't go their way or they face some kind of adversity. Instead of persevering, they get all bent out of shape. Before long they're down and discouraged, which is understandable, especially when we've struggled with a problem or a weakness for a long time. It's not unusual to come to a place where we acquiesce.

But you have to be more determined than that. The fifth step to living at our full potential is finding strength through adversity. Our circumstances in life may occasionally knock us down or force us to sit down for a while, but we must not stay down. The good news is, you don't have to stay down. Even if you can't see up on the outside, get up on the inside. Have that victor's attitude and mentality. Stay with an attitude of faith.

Set your face like a flint and say, "God, I may not understand this, but I know You are still in control. And You said all things would work together for my good. You said You would take this evil and turn it around and use it to my advantage. So Father, I thank You that You are going to bring me through this!" No matter what you may face in life, if you know how to get up on the inside, adversities cannot keep you down.

Keep on getting up in your heart, mind, and will.

The steps of a good man are ordered by the LORD:
and he delighteth in his way.
PSALM 37:23 KJV

Encourage Yourself in the Lord

To live your best life now, you must act on your will, not simply your emotions. Sometimes that means you have to take steps of faith even when you are hurting, grieving, or still reeling from an attack of the enemy.

Before David became king of Israel, he and his men returned home to find their city had been attacked, their homes burned, their possessions stolen, and their women and children kidnapped. Instead of sitting around devastated and mourning over what had been lost, David encouraged himself in the Lord and convinced his men to attack the enemy. As they persevered, God supernaturally helped them to recover everything that had been stolen.

You may be sitting around waiting for God to change your circumstances. *Then* you're going to be happy; *then* you're going to have a good attitude; *then* you're going to give God praise. But God is waiting for you to get up on the inside as David did. It will take courage; it will definitely take determination, but you can do it if you decide to do so.

God wants you to be a winner, not a whiner. Don't allow yourself to wave the white flag of surrender. You must show the enemy that you're more determined than he is. Shout aloud if you must, "I'm going to stand in faith even if I have to stand my whole lifetime!" When you do your part, God will begin to change things and work supernaturally in your life.

Develop a victor's mentality and watch what God begins to do.

David was greatly distressed because the people spoke of stoning him . . . But David strengthened himself in the Lord his God.

1 SAMUEL 30:6 NASB

Do not throw away your confidence; it will be richly rewarded.

Hebrews 10:35

In everything give thanks; for this is God's will for you in Christ Jesus.

1 Thessalonians 5:18 NASB

The Lord sustains all who fall and raises up all who are bowed down.

Psalm 145:14 NASB

A Determined Spirit

Friend, life is too short to trudge through it depressed and defeated. No matter what has come against you or what is causing you to slip and fall, no matter who or what is trying to push you down, you need to keep getting up on the inside. If you want to give your enemy a nervous breakdown, learn to keep a good attitude even when the bottom drops out! Learn to be happy even when things don't go your way.

When many people face adversity, they allow their doubt to cloud their determination, thus weakening their faith. They don't persevere; they don't keep a good attitude. Ironically, because their spirits are not right, they remain in bad situations longer than necessary. Medical science tells us that people with a determined, feisty spirit get well quicker than people who are prone to be negative and discouraged. That's because God made us to be determined. We were not created to live in depression and defeat. A negative spirit dries up your energy; it weakens your immune system. Many people are living with physical ailments and emotional bondages because they are not standing up on the inside.

Get rid of the mind-set that's saying you can't do it; you can't be happy; you have too much to overcome. Those are all lies from the enemy. Learn to tap into the can-do power that God has placed inside you. Stand strong and fight the good fight of faith.

Everyone has a reason to give God thanks.

For the vision is yet for an appointed time; but at the end it will speak, and it will not lie. Though it tarries, wait for it; because it will surely come, it will not tarry.

HABAKKUK 2:3 NKJV

Let us then approach the throne of grace with confidence, so that we may receive mercy and find grace to help us in our time of need.

HEBREWS 4:16

Trust God's Timing

Human nature tends to want everything right now. When we pray for our dreams to come to pass, we want them to be fulfilled immediately. But we have to understand, God has an appointed time to answer our prayers and to bring our dreams to pass. And the truth is, no matter how badly we want it sooner, it's not going to change His appointed time.

When we misunderstand God's timing, we live upset and frustrated, wondering when God is going to do something. But when you understand God's timing, you won't live all stressed out. You can relax knowing that God is in control, and at the "appointed time" He is going to make it happen. It may be next week, next year, or ten years from now. But whenever it is, you can rest assured it will be in God's timing.

God is not like an ATM machine, where you punch in the right codes and receive what you requested. Prayers are not always answered within twenty-four hours. No, we all have to wait and learn to trust God. The key is, are we going to wait with a good attitude and expectancy, knowing God is at work whether we can see anything happening or not? We need to know that behind the scenes, God is putting all the pieces together. And one day, at the appointed time, you will see the culmination of everything that God has been doing.

God often works the most when we see it and feel it the least.

But I trust in you, O Lord; I say, "You are my God."
My times are in your hands.
Psalm 31:14–15

I have learned to be content whatever the circumstances.
Philippians 4:11

Be Content

David had a big dream for his life. He had a desire to make a difference, but as a young man he spent many years as a shepherd, caring for his father's sheep. I'm sure there were plenty of times when he was tempted to think that God had forgotten him. He must have thought, *God, what am I doing here? There's no future in this place. When are You going to change this situation?* But David understood God's timing. He knew that if he would be faithful in obscurity, God would promote him at the right time. He knew God would bring his dreams to pass in due season.

You know the story. God brought David out of those fields, he defeated Goliath, and eventually he was made king of Israel.

Perhaps you have a big dream in your heart—a dream to have a better marriage, to own your own business, to help hurting people—but like David, you don't really see any human way your dream could happen.

I have good news for you! God isn't limited to natural, human ways of doing things. If you will trust God and keep a good attitude, staying faithful right where you are and not getting in a hurry and trying to force things to happen, God will promote you at the right time, in your due season. He will bring your dreams to pass. Rest in Him!

Contentment starts in your attitude.

God Sees the Big Picture

We don't always understand God's methods. His ways don't always make sense to us, but we have to realize that God sees the big picture. Consider this possibility: You may be ready for what God has for you, but somebody else who is going to be involved is not ready yet. God has to do a work in another person or another situation before your prayer can be answered according to God's will for your life. All the pieces have to come together for it to be God's perfect time.

But never fear; God is getting everything lined up in your life. You may not feel it; you may not see it. Your situation may look just as it did for the past ten years, but then one day, in a split second of time, God will bring it all together. When it is God's timing, all the forces of darkness can't stop Him. When it's your due season, God will bring it to pass.

To live your best life now, you must learn to trust God's timing. You can be sure that right now, God is arranging all the pieces to come together to work out His plan for your life. He has been working in your favor long before you encountered the problem. Don't grow impatient and try to force doors to open. Don't try to make things happen in your own strength. The answer will come, and it will be right on time.

Let God do it His way.

Let us not become weary in doing good, for at the proper time we will reap a harvest if we do not give up.
Galatians 6:9

"For my thoughts are not your thoughts, neither are your ways my ways," declares the Lord. "As the heavens are higher than the earth, so are my ways higher than your ways and my thoughts than your thoughts."
Isaiah 55:8–9

"But he knows the way that I take; when he has tested me, I will come forth as gold."

Job 23:10

Beloved, do not be surprised at the fiery ordeal among you, which comes upon you for your testing, as though some strange thing were happening to you.

1 Peter 4:12 NASB

Tests of Faith

When adversity comes knocking at the door or calamities occur, some people immediately think they have done something wrong, that God surely must be punishing them. They don't understand that God has a divine purpose for every challenge that comes into our lives. He doesn't send problems, but sometimes He allows us to go through them.

Why is that? The Bible says temptations, trials, and difficulties must come, because if we are to strengthen our spiritual muscles and grow stronger, we must have adversities to overcome and attacks to resist. Trials are intended to test our character, to test our faith. If you will learn to cooperate with God and be quick to change and correct the areas He brings to light, then you'll pass that test and be promoted to a new level.

God often allows you to go through difficult situations to draw out those impurities in your character. You can pray and resist it, but it's not going to do any good. God is more interested in changing you than He is in changing the circumstances. He will put people and circumstances in your path that grate on you like sandpaper, but He will use them to rub off your rough edges. You may not always like it; you may want to run from it; you may even resist it, but God is going to keep bringing up the issue again and again until you pass the test.

Work with God in the refining process rather than fighting against Him.

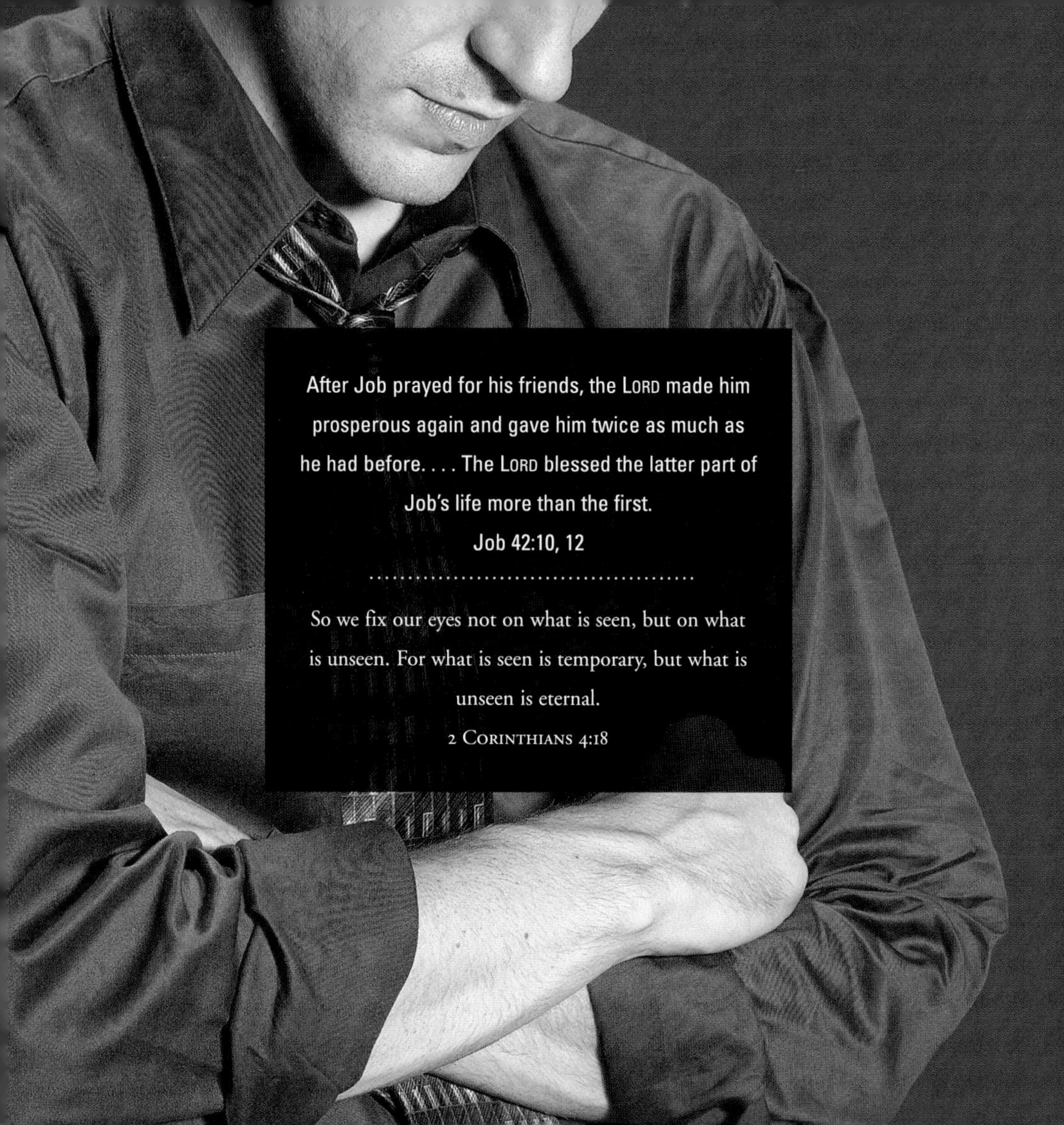

After Job prayed for his friends, the LORD made him prosperous again and gave him twice as much as he had before. . . . The LORD blessed the latter part of Job's life more than the first.

Job 42:10, 12

So we fix our eyes not on what is seen, but on what is unseen. For what is seen is temporary, but what is unseen is eternal.

2 CORINTHIANS 4:18

In the Bible, we read of Job, a good man who loved God and had a heart to do what's right. Yet in a few weeks' time, he lost his business, his flocks and herds, his family, and his health. Things could not get any worse for Job, and I'm sure he was tempted to be bitter. He could have said, "God, it's not fair. I don't understand why this is happening to me."

His own wife told him, "Job, just curse God and die."

But no, Job knew that God is a God of restoration. He knew God could turn any situation around. And his attitude was, *Even if I die I'm going to die trusting God. I'm going to die believing for the best.* And, when it was all said and done, God not only turned Job's calamity around, He brought Job out with twice that he had before.

I've discovered two kinds of faith—a *delivering* faith and a *sustaining* faith. Delivering faith is when God instantly turns your situation around. When that happens, it's great. But it takes a greater faith and a deeper walk with God to have sustaining faith. Sustaining faith is what gets you through those dark nights of the soul when, like Job, you don't know where to go or what to do . . . but because of your faith in God, you do. Faith tells us the best is yet to come.

DEVELOP A RESTORATION MENTALITY.

LIVE
TO GIVE

God is a giver,

and if you want Him to pour out

His blessing and favor in your life,

then you must learn to be

a giver and not a taker.

Remember the words of the Lord Jesus, how he said, It is more blessed to give than to receive.

ACTS 20:35 KJV

For God so loved the world, that he gave his only begotten Son.

JOHN 3:16 KJV

We Were Created to Give

Many people nowadays are blatantly and unashamedly living for themselves. Society teaches us to look out for number one. "What's in it for me?" We readily acknowledge this as the "me" generation, and that same narcissism sometimes spills over into our relationship with God, our families, and one another. Ironically, this selfish attitude condemns us to living shallow, unrewarding lives. No matter how much we acquire for ourselves, we are never satisfied.

One of the greatest challenges we face in our quest to enjoy our best lives now is the temptation to live selfishly. Because we believe that God wants the best for us, and that He wants us to prosper, it is easy to slip into the subtle trap of selfishness. Not only will you avoid that pitfall, but you will have more joy than you dreamed possible when you live to give, which is the sixth step to living at your full potential.

God is a giver, and if you want to experience a new level of God's joy, if you want Him to pour out His blessing and favor in your life, then you must learn to be a giver and not a taker. We were not made to function as self-involved people, thinking only of ourselves. No, God created us to be givers. And you will never be truly fulfilled as a human being until you learn the simple secret of how to give your life away.

Have an attitude that says, Who can I bless today?

No "Lone Rangers"

You may not realize it, but it is extremely selfish to go around always dwelling on your problems, always thinking about what you want or need, and hardly noticing the many needs of others all around you. One of the best things you can do if you're having a problem is to help solve somebody else's problem. If you want your dreams to come to pass, help someone else fulfill his or her dreams. Start sowing some seeds so God can bring you a harvest.

We were created to give, not to simply please ourselves. If you miss that truth, you will miss the abundant, overflowing, joy-filled life that God has in store for you. But when we reach out to other people in need, God will make sure that your own needs are supplied. If you're down and discouraged, get your mind off yourself and go help meet someone else's need. Sow the seed that will bring you a harvest.

Perhaps you feel you have nothing to give. Sure you do! You can give a smile or a hug. You can do some menial but meaningful task to help someone. You can visit someone in the hospital or make a meal for a person who is shut in. You can write an encouraging letter. Somebody needs what you have to share. Somebody needs your friendship. God created us to be free, but He didn't make us to function as "Lone Rangers." We need one another.

GOD WILL NOT FILL A CLOSED FIST WITH GOOD THINGS.

"Assuredly, I say to you, inasmuch as you did it to one of the least of these My brethren, you did it to Me."

Matthew 25:40 NKJV

ONE MAN GIVES FREELY, YET GAINS EVEN MORE; ANOTHER WITHHOLDS UNDULY, BUT COMES TO POVERTY.

PROVERBS 11:24

See that none of you repays another with evil for evil, but always aim to show kindness and seek to do good to one another and to everybody.
1 Thessalonians 5:15 AMP

"Love your enemies, do good to those who hate you, bless those who curse you, and pray for those who spitefully use you."
LUKE 6:27–28 NKJV

Walk in Love

How you treat other people can have a great impact on the degree of blessings and favor of God you will experience in your life. Are you good to people? Are you kind and considerate? Do you speak and act with love in your heart and regard other people as valuable and special? Friend, you can't treat people poorly and expect to be blessed.

The Bible says we are to "aim to show kindness and seek to do good." We must be proactive. We should be on the lookout to share His mercy, kindness, and goodness with people. Moreover, we need to be kind and do good to people even when somebody is unkind to us.

When somebody doesn't treat you right, you have a golden opportunity to help heal a wounded heart. Keep in mind, hurting people often hurt other people as a result of their own pain. If somebody is rude or inconsiderate, you can almost be certain that they have some unresolved issues inside. The last thing they need is for you to respond angrily.

Keep taking the high road and be kind and courteous. Walk in love and have a good attitude. God sees what you're doing, and He is our vindicator. He will make sure your good actions and attitude will overcome that evil. If you'll keep doing the right thing, you will come out far ahead of where you would have been had you fought fire with fire.

Evil is never overcome by more evil.

"As for you, you meant evil against me, but God meant it for good in order to bring about this present result, to preserve many people alive."

GENESIS 50:20 NASB

Love (God's love in us) does not insist on its own rights or its own way, for it is not self-seeking; it is not touchy or fretful or resentful; it takes no account of the evil done to it [it pays no attention to a suffered wrong].

1 CORINTHIANS 13:5 AMP

Love Overcomes Evil

If anybody had a right to return evil instead of love, it was Joseph. His brothers hated him so much, they purposed to kill him but then sold him into slavery. Years went by, and Joseph experienced all sorts of troubles and heartaches. But Joseph kept a good attitude, and God continued to bless him. After thirteen years of being in prison for a crime he didn't commit, God supernaturally promoted him to the second highest position in Egypt.

When Joseph's brothers came to Egypt and suddenly found their lives were in Joseph's hands, can you imagine the fear that gripped their hearts? This was Joseph's opportunity to pay them back. Yet Joseph extended his mercy. Is it any wonder he was so blessed with God's favor? Joseph knew how to treat people right.

You may have people in your life who have done you great wrong, and you have a right to be angry and bitter. You may feel as though your whole life has been stolen away by somebody. But if you will choose to let go of your grudge and forgive them, you can overcome that evil with good. You can get to the point where you can look at the people who have hurt you and return good for evil. If you do that, God will pour out His favor in your life in a fresh way. He will honor you; He will reward you, and He'll make those wrongs right.

God wants His people to help heal wounded hearts.

Live in harmony with one another; be sympathetic, love as brothers, be compassionate and humble.

1 PETER 3:8

If anyone . . . sees his brother and fellow believer in need, yet closes his heart of compassion against him, how can the love of God live and remain in him?

1 JOHN 3:17 AMP

Keep an Open Heart

Everywhere you go these days people are hurting and discouraged; many have broken dreams. They've made mistakes; their lives are in a mess. They need to feel God's compassion and His unconditional love. They don't need somebody to judge and criticize them. They need somebody to bring hope, to bring healing, to show God's mercy. Really, they are looking for a friend, somebody who will be there to encourage them, who will take the time to listen to their story and genuinely care.

Our world is crying out for people with compassion, people who love unconditionally, people who will take some time to help their fellow sojourners on this planet. Certainly, when God created us, He put His supernatural love in all of our hearts. He's placed in you the potential to have a kind, caring, gentle, loving spirit. Because you are created in God's image, you have the moral capacity to experience God's compassion in your heart.

If you want to live your best life now, you must make sure that you keep your heart of compassion open. We need to be on the lookout for people we can bless. We need to be willing to be interrupted and inconvenienced if it means we can help meet somebody else's need. You have the opportunity to make a difference in that person's life. You must learn to follow that love. Don't ignore it. Act on it. Somebody needs what you have.

This world is desperate to experience the love and compassion of our God.

The Compassion of Jesus

If you study the life of Jesus, you will discover that He always took time for people. He was never too busy with His own agenda, with His own plans. He wasn't so caught up in Himself that He was unwilling to stop and help a person in need. He could have easily said, "Listen, I'm busy. I have a schedule to keep." But no, Jesus had compassion on people. He was concerned about what they were going through, and He willingly took time to meet their needs. He freely gave of His life. I believe He demands nothing less from those who claim to be His followers today.

If you want to experience God's abundant life, you must start taking time to help other people. Sometimes if we would just take the time to listen to people, we could help initiate a healing process in their lives. So many people have pain bottled up inside them. They have nobody they can talk to; they don't trust anybody. If you can open your heart of compassion and be that person's friend—without judging or condemning—and simply have an ear to listen, you may help lift that heavy burden.

More than our advice, more than our instruction, people need somebody with whom they can be honest, a friend they can count on. You will be amazed at what a positive impact you can have if you will just learn to be a good listener.

Learn to follow the flow of God's divine love.

When [Jesus] saw the crowds, he had compassion on them, because they were harassed and helpless, like sheep without a shepherd. Then he said to his disciples, "The harvest is plentiful but the workers are few. Ask the Lord of the harvest, therefore, to send out workers into his harvest field."

MATTHEW 9:36–38

Filled with compassion, Jesus reached out his hand and touched the man. "I am willing," he said. "Be clean!" Immediately the leprosy left him and he was cured.

MARK 1:41

A generous man will prosper;
he who refreshes others will
himself be refreshed.
Proverbs 11:25

God Loves a Cheerful Giver

The reason many people are not growing is because they are not sowing. They are living self-centered lives. Unless they change their focus and start reaching out to others, they will probably remain in a depressed condition, emotionally, financially, socially, and spiritually.

All through the Bible, we find the principle of sowing and reaping. "Whatever a man sows, that he will also reap" (Gal. 6:7 NKJV). Just as a farmer must plant some seed if he hopes to reap a harvest, we, too, must plant some good seed in the fields of our families, careers, businesses, and personal relationships. If you want to reap happiness, you have to sow some "happiness" seeds by making others happy. If you want to reap financial blessing, you must sow financial seeds in the lives of others. The seed always has to lead.

In the midst of a great famine in the land of Canaan, Isaac did something that people without insight may have thought rather odd. He sowed seed and then reaped a hundredfold crop, because the Lord blessed him (Gen. 26:12). In his time of need, Isaac didn't wait around, expecting someone else to come to his rescue. No, he acted in faith, and God supernaturally multiplied that seed.

Maybe you're in some sort of famine today. It could be a financial famine; or maybe you're simply famished for friends. Whatever the need, sow some seeds and reap a huge harvest.

In the time of need, sow a seed.

He who sows sparingly and grudgingly will also reap sparingly and grudgingly, and he who sows generously [that blessings may come to someone] will also reap generously and with blessings. . . . God loves (He takes pleasure in, prizes above other things, and is unwilling to abandon or do without) a cheerful (joyous, "prompt to do it") giver [whose heart is in his giving].

2 Corinthians 9:6–7 AMP

We Were Created to Give

Many people nowadays are blatantly and unashamedly living for themselves. Society teaches us to look out for number one. "What's in it for me?" We readily acknowledge this as the "me" generation, and that same narcissism sometimes spills over into our relationship with God, our families, and one another. Ironically, this selfish attitude condemns us to living shallow, unrewarding lives. No matter how much we acquire for ourselves, we are never satisfied.

One of the greatest challenges we face in our quest to enjoy our best lives now is the temptation to live selfishly. Because we believe that God wants the best for us, and that He wants us to prosper, it is easy to slip into the subtle trap of selfishness. Not only will you avoid that pitfall, but you will have more joy than you dreamed possible when you live to give, which is the sixth step to living at your full potential.

God is a giver, and if you want to experience a new level of God's joy, if you want Him to pour out His blessing and favor in your life, then you must learn to be a giver and not a taker. We were not made to function as self-involved people, thinking only of ourselves. No, God created us to be givers. And you will never be truly fulfilled as a human being until you learn the simple secret of how to give your life away.

Have an attitude that says, Who can I bless today?

God is able to make all grace (every favor and earthly blessing) come to you in abundance, so that you may always and under all circumstances and whatever the need be self-sufficient [possessing enough to require no aid or support and furnished in abundance for ever good work and charitable donation].

2 CORINTHIANS 9:8 AMP

Give generously, for your gifts will return to you later. Divide your gifts among many, for in the days ahead you yourself may need much help.

ECCLESIASTES 11:1–2 TLB

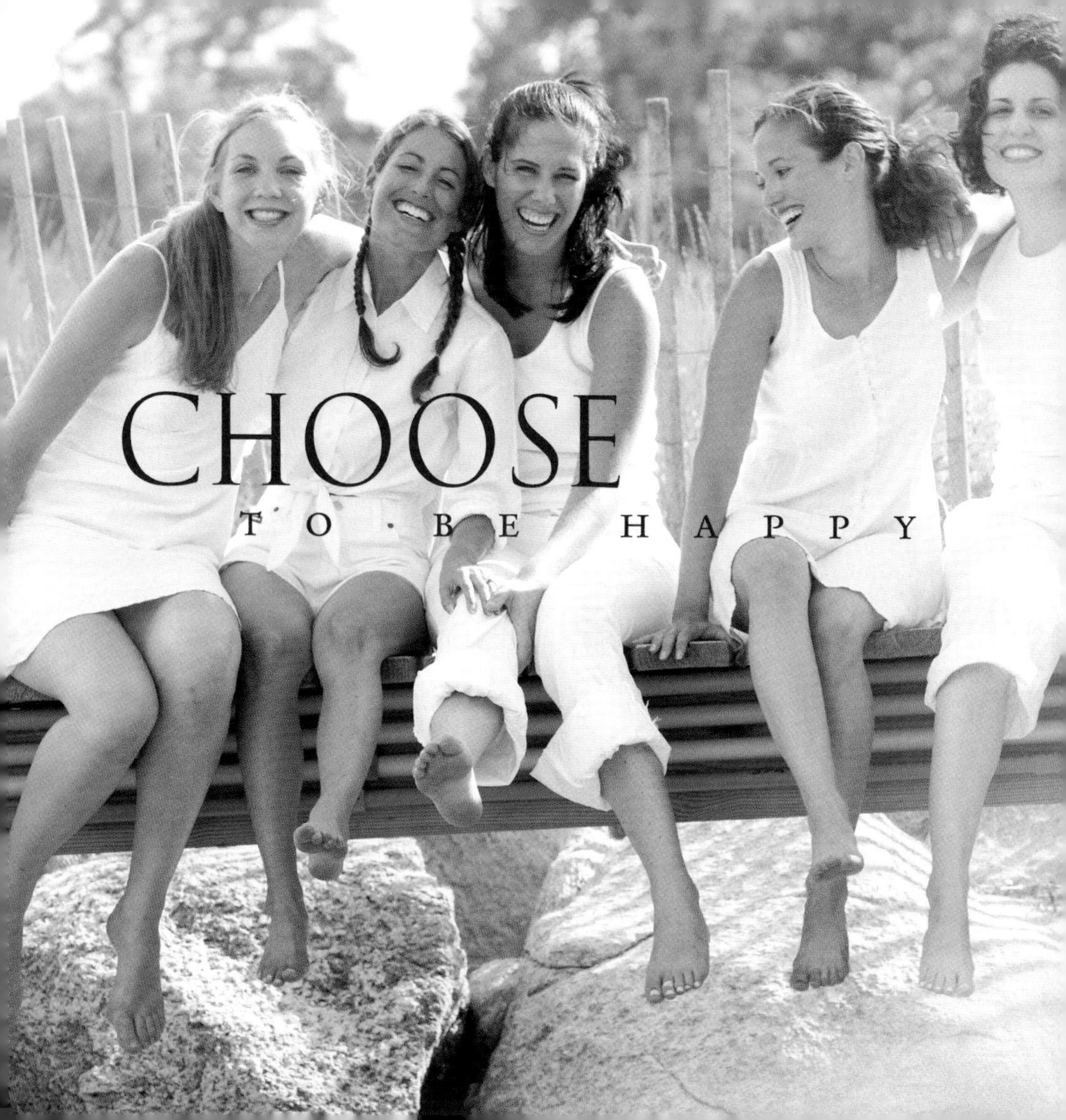
CHOOSE
TO · BE HAPPY

Learn to live one day at a time.

By an act of your will,

choose to start enjoying your

life right now.

Enjoy everything in your life.

This is the day which the LORD has made; let us rejoice and be glad in it.

PSALM 118:24 NASB

"Peace I leave with you; My peace I give to you; not as the world gives do I give to you. Do not let your heart be troubled, nor let it be fearful."

JOHN 14:27 NASB

Happiness Is Your Choice

It is a simple yet profound truth: Happiness is a choice. You don't have to wait for everything to be perfect in your family or with your business. You don't have to forgo happiness until you lose weight, break an unhealthy habit, or accomplish all your goals. The seventh step to enjoying your best life now is to choose to be happy today.

You might as well choose to be happy and enjoy your life! When you do that, not only will you feel better, but your faith will cause God to show up and work wonders. To do so, you must learn to live in today, one day at a time; better yet, make the most of this moment. It's good to set goals and make plans, but if you're always living in the future, you're never really enjoying the present in the way God wants us to.

We need to understand that God gives us the grace to live today. He has not yet given us tomorrow's grace, and we should not worry about it. Learn to live one day at a time. By an act of your will, choose to start enjoying your life right now. Learn to enjoy your family, friends, health, and work; enjoy everything in your life. Happiness is a decision you make, not an emotion you feel. God gives us His peace on the inside, but it's up to us to tap into God's supernatural peace. Happiness is your choice.

LIFE IS TOO SHORT NOT TO ENJOY EVERY SINGLE DAY.

Joy Is Your Strength

The apostle Paul wrote more than half of the New Testament while incarcerated, often in prison cells not much bigger than a small bathroom. Some historians and Bible commentators believe that the raw sewage system of that day ran right through one of the dungeons in which he was imprisoned. Yet Paul wrote such amazing faith-filled words as, "I can do all things through Christ who strengthens me" (Phil. 4:13 NKJV). And, "Thanks be to God, who always causes us to triumph," and "Rejoice in the Lord always. Again I will say, rejoice!" (Phil. 4:4 NKJV). Notice that we are to rejoice and be happy at all times. In your difficulties, when things aren't going your way, make a decision to stay full of joy.

We need to understand that the enemy is not really after your dreams, your health, or your finances. He's not primarily after your family. He's after your joy. The Bible says that "the joy of the LORD is your strength" (Neh. 8:10 NKJV), and your enemy knows if he can deceive you into living down in the dumps and depressed, then you are not going to have the necessary strength—physically, emotionally, or spiritually—to withstand his attacks.

When you rejoice in the midst of your difficulties, you're giving the enemy a black eye. He doesn't know what to do with people who keep giving God praise despite their circumstances. Make your choice to enjoy your life to the fullest today.

LEARN HOW TO SMILE AND LAUGH. QUIT BEING SO UPTIGHT AND STRESSED OUT.

A happy heart makes the face cheerful . . . the cheerful heart has a continual feast.

PROVERBS 15:13, 15

A cheerful heart is good medicine,
but a crushed spirit dries up the bones.

PROVERBS 17:22

WHATEVER YOU DO, DO YOUR WORK HEARTILY, AS FOR THE LORD RATHER THAN FOR MEN, KNOWING THAT FROM THE LORD YOU WILL RECEIVE THE REWARD OF THE INHERITANCE. IT IS THE LORD CHRIST WHOM YOU SERVE.

COLOSSIANS 3:23–24 NASB

Do you see a man who excels in his work? He will stand before kings; he will not stand before unknown men.

PROVERBS 22:29 NKJV

Be a Person of Excellence

For many people, mediocrity is the norm; they want to do as little as they possibly can and still get by. But God did not create us to be mediocre. He doesn't want us to just barely get by, or to do what everybody else is doing. God has called us to be people of excellence and integrity. Indeed, the only way to be truly happy is to live with excellence and integrity. Any hint of compromise will taint our greatest victories or our grandest achievements.

A person of excellence and integrity goes the extra mile to do what's right. He keeps his word even when it's difficult. People of excellence give their employers a full day's work; they don't come in late, leave early, or call in sick when they are not. When you have an excellent spirit, it shows up in the quality of your work, and the attitude with which you do it.

God's people are people of excellence. Remember: You represent Almighty God. How you live, how you conduct your business and do your work, is all a reflection on our God. If you want to live your best life now, start aiming for excellence in everything you do. Whatever we do, we should give our best effort and do it as if we were doing it for God. If we'll work with that standard in mind, God promises to reward us, and others will be attracted to our God.

Subtle compromises of excellence will keep you from God's best.

"Whoever can be trusted with very little can also be trusted with much, and whoever is dishonest with very little will also be dishonest with much."

LUKE 16:10

Quick! Catch all the little foxes before they ruin the vineyard of your love, for the grapevines are all in blossom.

SONG OF SOLOMON 2:15 NLT

Be a Person of Integrity

God wants us to be people of integrity, people of honor, people who are trustworthy. A person of integrity is open and honest and true to his word. He doesn't have any hidden agendas or ulterior motives. He doesn't need a legal contract to force him to fulfill his commitments. People of integrity are the same in private as they are in public. They do what's right whether anybody is watching or not.

If you don't have integrity, you will never reach your highest potential. Integrity is the foundation on which a truly successful life is built. Every time you compromise, every time you are less than honest, you are causing a slight crack in the foundation. If you continue compromising, that foundation will never be able to hold what God wants to build. You'll never have lasting prosperity if you don't first have integrity. You may enjoy some temporary success, but you'll never see the fullness of God's favor if you don't take the high road and make the more excellent choices. On the other hand, God's blessings will overtake us if we settle for nothing less than living with integrity.

God will only trust us with more after we have been faithful with a little. Remember, our lives are an open book before God. He looks at our hearts and motives. There's no limit to what God will do in your life when He knows that He can trust you.

Be willing to pay the price to do the right thing.

"He who believes in Me, as the Scripture has said, out of his heart will flow rivers of living water."

JOHN 7:38 NKJV

Never Take God for Granted

Living your best life now is living with enthusiasm and being excited about the life God has given you. It is believing for more good things in the days ahead, but it is also living in the moment and enjoying it to the hilt!

Let's not be naïve. The pressures, tensions, and stress of modern life constantly threaten to take a toll on our enthusiasm. You probably know some people who have lost their passion. They've lost their zest for life. Once they were excited about the future, but they've lost their fire.

The word *enthusiasm* derives from two Greek words, *en theos*, meaning "inspired by God." One of the main reasons we lose our enthusiasm in life is because we start to take for granted what God has done for us. We get accustomed to His goodness; it becomes routine.

Don't take for granted the greatest gift of all that God has given you—Himself! Don't allow your relationship with Him to become stale or your appreciation for His goodness to become common. We need to stir ourselves up, to replenish our supply of God's good gifts on a daily basis. Like the Israeli people in the wilderness who had to gather God's miraculous provisions of manna afresh each morning, we, too, cannot get by on yesterday's supply. We need fresh enthusiasm each day. Our lives need to be inspired, infused, filled afresh with God's goodness every day.

Stay filled with hope.

YOUR BEST LIFE NOW

God's people should be the happiest people on earth! So happy, in fact, that other people notice. Why? Because we not only have a fabulous future, we can enjoy life today! That's what living your best life now is all about.

Don't just go through the motions in life. Make a decision that you are not going to live another day without the joy of the Lord in your life; without love, peace, and passion; without being excited about your life. And understand that you don't have to have something extraordinary happening in your life to be excited. You may not have the perfect job or the perfect marriage or live in the perfect environment, but you can still choose to live each day aglow with God's presence.

Friend, if you want to see God's favor, do everything with your whole heart. Do it with passion and some fire. Give it your all. Not only will you feel better, but that fire will spread, and soon other people will want what you have. Wherever you are in life, make the most of it and be the best you can be.

Raise your level of expectancy. It's our faith that activates the power of God. Let's quit limiting Him with our small-minded thinking and start believing Him for bigger and better things. God will take you places you've never dreamed of, and you will be having your best life now.

STAY PASSIONATE ABOUT SEEING YOUR DREAMS COME TO PASS.

Never lag in zeal and in earnest endeavor; be aglow and burning with the Spirit, serving the Lord.

ROMANS 12:11 AMP

Stir up (rekindle the embers of, fan the flame of, and keep burning) the [gracious] gift of God, [the inner fire] that is in you.

2 TIMOTHY 1:6 AMP